GLOBAL TALENT
TALENT
UNLEASHED

Dedication

This book is dedicated to everyone who devotes their own work to harnessing the talents of everyone, everywhere—for the betterment of us all. To our customers, our partners, and my Dream Team—your work, passion, and ingenuity inspire me!

CONTENTS

Foreword

Five years ago, our leadership team came up with an ambitious strategy for our 75-person company, Acceleration Partners: We were going to take our business global.

We are a premier agency in a highly specialized industry called affiliate, or partner, marketing. Previously, if you wanted to run an affiliate or partner program globally, it meant working with multiple agencies and software platforms across the world. However, the technology platforms in our industry were beginning to go global, and we believed the demand for global affiliate management services would soon follow. We began formulating a plan to build teams in both Europe and Asia and soon launched our business in both regions.

That is when the real work began. While we were correct in estimating where the market was headed, we could not have imagined the complexity that the process of going global would add to our business.

In addition to the cultural challenges of recruiting and hiring employees abroad, and extending our award-winning culture to different regions, we soon discovered just how onerous it could be to establish a legal presence in multiple foreign countries and onboard employees on the ground as a new entrant in these competitive markets. We were in over our heads and needed help. Specifically, we needed a partner.

It was during this period that one of our board members connected us with Nicole Sahin and her company, Globalization Partners. Globalization Partners created a game-changing global employment platform that makes it easy for companies like ours to hire anyone, anywhere, quickly, easily, and *legally*. Many businesses today are expanding globally with practices that openly violate local employment and tax laws. These companies are often blissfully ignorant of the significant risk and future liability they engender by taking a laissez-faire approach to global expansion.

Globalization Partners' platform enabled us to be nimble, and to build teams quickly in response to market demand. Nicole and I also became friends and peer advisors, sharing best practices from our respective experiences building remote teams and maintaining unified company cultures, something that is crucial for long-term success. Her experience and guidance in these areas were as invaluable as the services Globalization Partners provided us. Today, Acceleration Partners has over 200 employees globally. The bold bet we made five years ago is paying off for both our business and our customers, and our company is more diverse and dynamic than ever before.

As the world becomes smaller, the human experience, including at work, is becoming richer and more dynamic. This has put us in a paradox where companies are increasingly recognizing the value of building global teams, but also coming to understand how difficult it is to execute on their global ambitions from an administrative, logistical, and cultural standpoint.

In *Global Talent Unleashed*, Nicole will open your eyes to the rewards your business can reap from a global marketplace of talent. She will also walk you through the "how" of global expansion so you can learn from both the mistakes and best practices of companies that have gone on to make the model work for them.

If you are looking to tap into the new world of global talent, I cannot think of a more qualified guide to take you on this journey than my friend Nicole.

Robert Glazer
Founder and CEO, Acceleration Partners
Wall Street Journal and *USA Today* bestselling author of *Elevate*, *Friday Forward*, and *How to Thrive in the Virtual Workplace*

PREFACE

Globalization Partners exists, in part, because of my love of and appreciation for global travel, which was sparked during college. A series of opportunities to leave my hometown of St. Louis and travel to countries I had barely heard of was only possible thanks to my mom.

I have been so fortunate to receive so many gifts, from scholarships that enabled me to attend college, to a great family, to finding my soul mate, and, most recently, the gift of being able to create my own family. However, one gift in particular changed my life in a very profound way.

In 1997, I was a college freshman at Maryville University. I had chosen to stay close to home in part because of the full scholarship the university had offered, but also knowing that I would have the opportunity to study abroad through this institution. That potential for international adventure was everything I'd ever wanted. As excited as I was to go to college, I was even more excited to study abroad as part of that experience.

One day I came across a pamphlet for a semester-abroad program called Semester at Sea, which had been tucked in the back of a brochure rack in the university's dining hall. The University of

Virginia had converted a cruise ship into a floating classroom that circumnavigated the globe, stopping in 12 countries over 100 days, with three to five days in each country. Days in between were spent in classrooms focused on themes having to do with the countries students would be exploring. The list of countries included places I'd never even heard of. (Where was Malaysia?!)

I slid the pamphlet into my purse to show my mom the next time I went home. I was so intrigued by the concept of turning a boat into a classroom. As a family, we had gone to the Caribbean, but I had never traveled internationally to any extent and was excited by the possibilities such an experience might provide.

THE GIFT OF PLANNING

A few weeks later, my parents invited me to meet them at our favorite family restaurant—Gianino's—for a dinner, just the three of us. It was unusual for them to ask me to leave campus during the week, so I was curious about the request. Once we were together, nestled away in the back corner booth where my family always celebrated important occasions, my mom pulled the Semester at Sea brochure out of her purse. To be honest, I had forgotten all about it. It had been a fantasy—a trip I would have loved to have taken but didn't honestly think could happen for me.

That's when my mom told me a story.

I noticed she was nervous; she was holding my Dad's hand under the table for support. She told me that since my sister and I had been small children, she had set aside US$20 a week in a shoebox under her workshop table. One time, my dad had apparently found the shoebox and excitedly suggested they go on vacation! She quickly told him no. She didn't know what the money was for, she said, but she felt compelled to save for something. She was confident she would know what it was when she saw it.

That time was now. She had found what she was saving for all those years when I handed her that pamphlet. She wanted me to enroll in the Semester at Sea and, as only a loving parent could do, miraculously had manifested the means to enable the journey.

To say this was a gift that changed my life is the understatement of a century, not the least of which was because it was entirely unexpected. For the next several months, I worked extra side jobs before and after school to save up for expenses I would have on the trip. That in itself gifted me precious understanding of the value of money, and the value of work.

Then, several months later, my parents and sister traveled with me to the Bahamas to wave goodbye as the ship containing 600 students, a team of world-class professors, and I left port. It would be the journey of a lifetime.

THE GIFT OF SELF-AWARENESS

On board the ship three days later, after meeting various student representatives of the Communist Party of Cuba on the boat, we first docked in Cuba. We were part of the largest envoy of Americans to land in that country since the Bay of Pigs. Cuba was communist and extremely impoverished. To witness firsthand the impact of communist ideals, as presented by the students—combined with the extreme poverty caused by the American embargo only 90 miles from American shores—absolutely stunned me. I had never realized how privileged I was.

In addition to learning about the Cuban government and the country's economic situation, I witnessed the extraordinary joie de vivre of the Cuban people, their pride in their history, and their love for their families. My life changed in that moment, but my journey had just begun.

Over the next 100 days, I hitchhiked in Brazil; learned about racism and social change by witnessing South Africa in its early years post-Apartheid; stood in awe of the vast, wild plains of the Serengeti; observed the challenges of land conservation in Kenya; soaked in the vibrant colors and kicked up clouds of jasmine while following a barefoot tour guide named Benny, who escorted me through his Dalit village in India; and celebrated an impromptu spring break with my friends and a young, newly married Muslim woman in full hijab who shared stories about dating customs in Malaysia.

As the sun rose and the boat travelled up the Mekong Delta into Vietnam, I reflected on how my father, as a young soldier, had taken the same route 30 years earlier and under entirely different circumstances. I experienced Shanghai at the beginning of its ascent into the superpower China is now. I grieved and avoided protestors when

America bombed the Chinese embassy in Belgrade. I partook in the ancient traditions of Kyoto, Japan.

By the time I sailed home, 100 days later, my life, my personality, and my mind had been broken wide open. I no longer fit the American Midwest lifestyle that I had been brought up in. All of my efforts in the classroom that had gotten me to that point had been eclipsed in 100 days by the reality of the immense, beautiful world that suddenly seemed so easy to explore.

I learned empathy for nearly everyone I met and became absolutely fearless about exploring—to learn the stories of people who were deemed different from me. I came to believe that if people could just meet—connect with other people around the world—it might be possible to unite the globe in a single generation. If we only saw just how much we had in common, how could we ever want to do anything but help each other succeed?

A VISION OF WHAT'S POSSIBLE

Fast forward 15 years and, after finishing my MBA, I joined a small consulting firm that was helping companies expand internationally. Within a short period of time, I was advising companies from Tesla to Infinera and helping them set up their subsidiaries and hire teams globally. I quickly became the top rainmaker for the firm, helping it to grow to 200 employees in six years, and managed two regions of the firm from an operations perspective.

In that time, I started to see patterns emerge. Customers were always facing the same problems, which we would then address. We had to set up a whole new company in the country our customer was planning to hire teams in, including figuring out the human resource procedures and regulations, legal requirements, and tax processes, all before they could even hire their first worker. It was extremely complicated and the likelihood of getting something wrong along the way was high, even with a world-class team (like ours) retained to support them.

After working through this process hundreds of times, I asked myself—what if I could set up a global megacorporation and give each customer access to hire its employees through it? The megacorporation would be the main company under which all customers could employ their own international team members. That would eliminate the need to repeatedly set up new entities for each and every customer, because they could leverage ours. Beyond that, we could build software on top of the global legal infrastructure, and make it truly easy to hire anyone, anywhere, quickly and easily.

With this new idea, I left the consulting firm and took a year off to travel the world, visiting 24 countries and verifying whether I could make my concept work along the way. When I returned, in 2012, I founded Globalization Partners, a firm that is fundamentally changing the way the world does business by enabling companies to bypass the international legal and infrastructure barriers that they normally encounter when going global.

The way it works varies by country, but in general, our customers identify the talent, and we add candidates to our locally compliant payroll, using an AI-driven customer interface software that makes it fast and easy for customers to engage global team members—without registering local branch offices in each location. The structure of delivering these services can vary on a country-by-country basis and depends on each country's laws and regulations.

Today we employ thousands of people on behalf of our customers in more than 187 countries. We were named one of the fastest growing companies in America in 2020 by the *Financial Times*, and have won more awards than we can count for building a company culture that people love. Our customer success rating is 98 percent, which was not shaken while we achieved our year-on-year exponential growth.

Most importantly, we've made it possible for companies everywhere to have access to top talent anywhere in the world by simplifying the process of hiring local employees. The reverse is also true—workers in all parts of the world can now connect with global employment opportunities, changing their quality of life and their family's. Barriers to entering the global workforce have been effectively demolished, as long as the individuals are sufficiently educated and have internet access.

In that way, Globalization Partners is striving to make an impact by building bridges between cultures and companies, connecting smart people around the world with opportunities for employment and business growth. Everyone, everywhere, should have access to good jobs in the new era of global remote work. Our team is honored to be part of accelerating the ability of people worldwide to meet their full potential.

It's my personal mission to break down barriers for and between people from all walks of life by breaking down barriers to global business. It began that first day my mom put US$20 into a shoebox, knowing someday it would fuel a larger purpose. The company I ultimately founded was born in large part due to my curiosity about the world and my desire to make an impact. Today, the company is on track to earn US$1 billion in annualized recurring revenue by the end of 2021; our internal team reports extremely high levels of employee satisfaction, and our customers love us. And yet, we're just getting started.

I hope this book enables you to do the same by helping you build the team of your dreams. The world is full of talent, and in the era of global remote work, it's at your fingertips.

Nicole M. Sahin
California, USA
August 2021

INTRODUCTION

Higher revenue. Improved profits. Greater market share. Lower cost structure. Product lifecycle extensions. Easier access to experienced talent pools. Experienced boots on the ground. These are just a handful of reasons organizations around the world continue to hire team members in new countries. For many, enhanced global reach is the linchpin in their corporate growth strategy. A quick look at the Fortune 500 bears this out, with companies on that impressive list averaging 317 international locations.[1]

Shareholders also reward companies that look globally for talent, according to *Chief Executive* magazine, in which a study of the 202 non-financial members of the Standard & Poor's 500 revealed that the high international growth group grew faster overall, diversified their revenue streams, improved their return on capital, and increased their reinvestment rate as the economy exited the great recession of 2008.[2] Then and now, an international mindset has been a catalyst for growth.

In fact, 87 percent of U.S.-based companies see international expansion as key to long-term growth, with 69 percent of those companies believing that emerging markets provide the greatest opportunities of all, reported Wells Fargo's 2016 Business Indicator.[3] In the tech sector, this push is even more evident, with global growth being the core focus of more than half the U.S. companies that received outside investment in 2019–2020.

For a majority of U.S. companies, global growth is their primary priority. The dominant factors that led companies to expand globally, according to CFO, included market share capture (50%), sales presence (45%), investment diversification (31%), ability to acquire top talent (29%), cost reduction (29%), mergers and acquisitions (28%), and to be located near a customer (22%).[4] Future-looking companies recognize that staying focused on local markets is limiting on several fronts.

THE INITIAL PUSH TO ENTER GLOBAL MARKETS

While the global opportunity has existed forever, only recent technological advances have made it possible for virtually any organization to do business globally, from Fortune 500 corporations to sole proprietors and mom and pop retailers. The doors are wide open for everyone, everywhere, and that's exciting.

What happened initially was something like the U.S. Gold Rush of the mid-1800s. After the widespread adoption of the internet, venture investors realized that the U.S. accounts for only about 26 percent of the world's economy, leaving close to 75 percent up for grabs by domestic-focused software companies. By expanding into Europe and Asia—which was suddenly much more realistic with faster telecommunications—companies could conceivably then capture 75 percent of the global market; they've effectively tripled their potential market size. This goal of expanding a company as large as possible is a very American ideal—one of our favorite expressions is "go big or go home." The result was that investors pushed U.S. companies to build global teams quickly.

The other pressure on American companies was copycats. U.S. companies recognized the need to move quickly to establish operations in other countries, to stake their claims and start marketing their products and services before local entrepreneurs there had time to effectively copy their business concepts. With ideas flying around the globe at the speed of light, companies realized they had a choice: either go capture that global market share quickly themselves or let a savvy local entrepreneur already on the ground take their idea and run with it. Take the case in point, Didi, the Uber of China, or Alibaba, the Amazon of China. Both are local incarnations of businesses that were started in the U.S. but whose executive teams were too slow to corner the market before a local entrepreneur copied their idea.

TECHNOLOGY OPENS NEW DOORS

The catalyst for this growth and expansion has been improvements in communications technology, which had a ripple effect on where, when, and how work was done. Those advancements made true remote work a reality. Employees can now be situated anywhere in the world—as long as they have connectivity.

Part of that shift has been triggered by the explosion in cellphone accessibility. According to Statista, as of January 2021, 5.25 billion people had mobile devices of some kind, or 67 percent of the global population.[5] It certainly feels like everyone everywhere has one, from C-suite executives in North America to farmers in Italy and tribesmen in Africa. The cellphone, in many ways, is becoming an equalizer—even if access to mobile devices, and indeed education, are not yet truly equal. Nonetheless, the cellphone has connected even remote parts of the world and made borderless commerce possible in a very short period of time.

Where business opportunities exist, people will migrate, including workers in search of opportunity and adventure. Increasing numbers of younger employees are opting to connect to work from unconventional locales, like the beach or the mountains.

Although younger generations of workers have expressed a preference for working outside of the office, whether at home or in a public place—"they are mostly interested in work flexibility,"[6] as author Dan Schawbel puts it—it wasn't until videoconferencing products like Zoom, WebEx, Google Meet, and Microsoft Teams allowed workers to remain truly connected from anywhere that the opportunity to earn a living from anywhere really took off.

Technology was the tipping point. There has always been global business, but the great leaps forward made by technology companies in the early 2000s sparked heightened interest in doing business globally. Suddenly, the idea that you could hire anyone, anywhere captured everyone's imagination. That led to a huge push toward outsourcing, first in China and then in India.

Unfortunately, there was a backlash following that initial foray into non-English-speaking countries. Consumer frustration following communication problems with some tech phone help agents caused many companies to backtrack and retrench to the safety of domestic shores. The move into those markets was too early to be done well, and it made some companies gun-shy.

What some have not yet realized is that, 10 or 15 years later, the market has totally changed. Whole cities have sprung up in countries like the Philippines, where nearly everyone works a flipped schedule to cater to North American customers. Phone and chat agents might sleep during the day, work at night, and enjoy happy hour at 5 a.m. instead of 5 p.m.—living a reverse lifestyle. Agents are also trained in the local accent and learn about local places and interests in the geographic area they serve, sometimes adopting a fictional persona to connect with callers; those fictional backstories may include details that suggest they attended the local high school or root for the major sports team in the area. Call centers in the Philippines help many agents to develop parallel identities that they use depending on which area the inbound caller is from. All this contributes to making outsourcing a viable option for their clientele.

However, some companies are shifting away from outsourcing and, instead, are now setting up their own local operations, employing their own local talent for this work. Others are using AI chatbots. Any time you have a service phone call, you might be talking with someone outside your home country or even a robot—whether you can identify it or not. Companies have gotten much better about this than they were in the "old days," around 10 years ago, when a challenging accent and bad training drove customers crazy. Now, customers don't even know when their customer support has been outsourced. If you ask whoever you're speaking with where they're located, they'll probably tell you they're in Montana, how the local sports team did that weekend, and a little about the local hunting season—all from their 3 a.m. perch in an Asian office park. It's amazing and impressive, and somewhat mind-boggling the first time you observe the quality of talent internationally.

WORKING REMOTELY HITS
ITS OWN TIPPING POINT

Just as interest in operating internationally was exploding, fueled by telecommunications and technology advances, remote work also took off. No longer did many white-collar workers have to be chained to a desk—they could work from virtually anywhere.

The onset of the 2020 pandemic added tremendous fuel to the remote work fire. Remote work went overnight from being a preference to a mandate; workers had to socially distance and still manage their work responsibilities. Most headed home to conduct work from a makeshift home office, some moved out of cities temporarily to more remote locations, but all who could were still working.

As of 2017, only 2.9 percent of the U.S. workforce, or 3.9 million employees, worked from home at least half the time, reported FlexJobs.[7] By late 2020, two-thirds of U.S. workers who had been working remotely during the pandemic expressed interest in continuing to do so, according to Gallup.[8] A larger Buffer study, also conducted in late 2020, found that 98 percent of the 3,500 workers surveyed stated an interest in working remotely at least some of the time throughout their careers,[9] and 77 percent of workers surveyed by Owl Labs said that, once we reach a post-pandemic stage, having the option to work from home would make them happier.[10] And to drive home the point that employees do want to be able to perform their jobs from home, that same Owl Labs study reported that 23 percent of full-time employees would take a pay cut of more than 10 percent if that's what it would take to be able to work from home at least some of the time.

It sounds like employers are listening. A recent study by CFO Research reported that three-quarters of executives say the Covid-19 pandemic fundamentally altered the way they think about hiring and workforce management, and 81 percent say it altered how they consider remote employees or the work-from-anywhere model.[11] More specifically, three-quarters of the survey respondents anticipate operating remote or hybrid workforce models by year-end 2022.

Why lease commercial space if a large percentage of your workforce would choose not to conduct work there? Many executives are asking this question, and frankly, those same executives don't want to go back to the office, either.

Despite the upheaval caused by the pandemic, most companies forged ahead with global hiring plans. Only 37 percent of the executives surveyed by CFO Research shut down their global hiring plans because of Covid-19, as of 2020.[12] Said another way, 63 percent were continuing to hire teams globally, though some indicated they would delay. At Globalization Partners, we've seen a huge surge in hiring internationally; companies have awakened to the opportunity to hire highly talented people everywhere, and what that means for the potential of their business. They're also hiring in different states across the U.S., lest our compatriots feel left out, and international companies are also hiring in the U.S.

GLOBAL HIRING CHALLENGES

Historically, expanding into new geographic markets has been a complex, lengthy, laborious process that gave many CEOs and CFOs pause. The local laws, human resource requirements, tax compliance processes, paperwork, restrictions—all of it made hiring even a single employee in another country extremely complicated and time-consuming. Unlike hiring within your own home country, where you can bring a new employee onboard almost instantaneously, hiring an employee in a new country could take up to six months or more. This is due primarily to the need to set up a company in that country before registering for payroll.

Hiring an employee in another jurisdiction the traditional way involves a number of steps for the employer, starting with registering as an employer in that country, paying taxes there, researching employment laws and required paperwork, beginning the recruitment of potential candidates, and then adding them to the payroll. It's a lengthy process that often leads employers to feel like their expansion plans have stalled.

Another major challenge is the fear associated with hiring an employee in another country. Aside from the hiring process itself, many companies are wary of bringing someone on board to represent their brand who is located halfway around the world, in some cases whom they've never met in person. How can they be sure the employee is even working?

Fortunately, that's one fear that may be dissipating, thanks to the sudden push to remote work during the pandemic.

SOCIETAL BENEFITS

Pre-pandemic, the concept of globalization implied that a physical office setup within a new country was a first step in a larger expansion plan. Today, although technology has made country borders almost irrelevant, location-driven growth is still the focus. Having a physical presence inside a country is still preferred—even required by some organizations—though the process for making that a reality can be much simpler.

Hiring employees in other countries just went mainstream and became a lot easier at the same time. That's good news, both for companies looking to expand and for potential employees looking for work.

This rising access to employment means an increase in opportunities for workers almost anywhere and, ultimately, a reduction in poverty globally. Access to employment opportunities means a rising average income. Where an estimated 30 percent of the world lived in extreme poverty around the year 2000, in 15 years that figure dropped to 10 percent.[13] We've accomplished so much in just one generation. The quality of life for people at the bottom of the economic spectrum has improved significantly, and the middle class has grown simultaneously.

Leveraging technology to connect with potential workers and provide income-earning opportunities is a major benefit of the global expansion push, on top of access to top talent, often at lower costs than were previously available. That push beyond U.S. borders is now easier, faster, and less costly for companies that aspire to tap into global markets. It is breaking down barriers and, ultimately, benefits us all.

PART I

Remote Work Is
Past the Tipping Point

The pace at which companies are expanding into new global markets has quickened dramatically in the last few years, in large part because of the rise of remote work.

With remote work having gone mainstream, the concept of workers on the payroll who are completing tasks many miles away from the home office is no longer suspect or concerning. The pandemic only helped confirm that employees can be just as productive, or more so, working from home or from space outside the office. Indeed, the advent of remote work accelerated a decade in just one year during the Covid-19 pandemic.

This increasing comfort with remote work has helped fuel interest in locating employees in offices around the world. And that's exactly what has happened—heightened demand for global employees.

CHAPTER 1

Now Is the Time to Go Global

DISTEK, INC.

Distek, Inc. provides laboratory instrumentation to the pharmaceutical and biotech industries from its New Jersey headquarters. Founded in 1976 by husband-and-wife duo Gerry and Pearl Brinker, the company is now run by their son Jeff and has more than 50 employees.

When Distek began its global expansion, it focused initially on the European (EU) market because it closely mimicked the U.S. market. The company has had great success in the EU region, primarily because of its first direct hire in partnership with Globalization Partners. Having a direct EU citizen presence based in Europe representing its interests and managing its distribution network keeps the whole Distek network focused on its products and the unique challenges of doing business outside of the U.S. Even more important, by hiring the EU individual via Globalization Partners, the company was able to minimize the legal, tax, and HR burdens traditionally associated with hiring in new countries.

> *With the legal, tax, and HR matters contracted via Globalization Partners, Distek's initial challenge of hiring globally was implementing the necessary technologies to allow office workers to perform their functions remotely. Microsoft Teams kept everyone connected and able to meet regularly to collaborate on projects.*
>
> *Establishing an early footprint outside of the U.S. allowed Distek to achieve significant growth and, ultimately, the company was able to shift its sales mix to nearly a 50:50 split between domestic and international markets—effectively doubling the market it was reaching by going global early.*

A wise woman once said, "Global commerce is the greatest enabler of global peace." That is, countries don't go to war with countries they have financial ties to; they protect them, because it's in their mutual best interest. To do otherwise is self-defeating. By forging global alliances and enabling global commerce, we're also building a more interconnected, sane, and calm world.

What countries, and companies, have in common is a goal to improve the economic wellbeing of their constituents, whether those are citizens, shareholders, or employees. The more interconnected our economies, the more we rely on each other to achieve our own goals.

As companies recognize the tremendous business opportunity beyond their own countries' borders, the push to expand internationally has been growing, often fueled by a desire to secure first-mover advantage in their industry or product category. Not that companies haven't been setting up shop in other countries before now—they have—but the power that comes with being first in a region and a product category has become evident. This decision is typically in support of a business directive to expand and grow geographically, and part of a bigger long-term vision for the company.

In some cases, however, the trigger is hiring an individual in another country, either because that person is a top performer the organization has been eyeing for years or because the company needs to establish a local office but has held off until locating a qualified employee. That is, the catalyst is the availability of talent located somewhere else but who is believed to be critical for the company's future growth. That professional's geographic location then spawns a larger-scale effort to grow the company from that one location.

Many companies have elected to delay hiring globally because of the horror stories they've heard about opening offices in other parts of the world. It was time-consuming and fraught with risks and dangers around every turn—enough to slow those growth plans. And they weren't wrong about the convoluted, expensive, lengthy process required to do business internationally.

THE OLD-SCHOOL EXPANSION PROCESS

Historically, the process of moving into another country looked something like this:

- Approach a U.S. law firm and ask for a referral to an attorney in your target country, which, let's say, is Australia.

- Then you do the same for an accountant—ask your local accountant for a referral to a skilled accountant there.

- Following the Australian attorney's advice, you would next decide which type of company structure to set up, a branch or a subsidiary, before you could hire or do business in Australia—and then form a new business entity within the country.

Those steps would trigger a number of subsequent steps, such as setting up a local bank account, which may then require that the major shareholder appear in person with their passport to prove their identity. Countries frequently require you to set up a bank account to reduce money laundering, and it has proved problematic for venture-backed businesses or companies with multiple shareholders, incidentally. This is also why I spent the first few years of running Globalization Partners flying around the globe to show up at bank offices with my passport in hand. Appearing in person is the only way to meet this requirement at many international banks.

Once you have a company up and running, you have to follow all the corporate laws in that country as well as the local employment laws, which differ entirely from the U.S. As part of your local company operations, you typically have to file annual tax filings and financial statements, which sometimes must be kept in the local language— this is true in China, for example. The risk of incorrectly structuring any of these legal documents is likely to have very significant tax consequences.

Some countries require that local companies have a local director, meaning a local resident who is employed by the company and a shareholder to some degree, who is responsible, or partially liable, for any of the business decisions. That requirement probably exists so that if the local government has a question about the company's operations, it has someone nearby it can turn to for explanations.

In some jurisdictions, you have to invest in an office—meaning you must financially commit to commercial space, or at least rent a mailing address—before the company can officially operate. In some parts of the world, vast rows of empty office spaces are leased solely to fulfill this requirement. To complete all of these steps and get the company legally set up could take anywhere from three to 12 months, depending on the country, and at least 10,000 emails back and forth, because the process has nuances and intricacies that are not intuitive. It's only once you've finished registering and setting up a local company in that country that you could start recruiting and hiring local employees.

When you are ready to hire and employ workers, it's time to decide what benefits you can and should offer them—and how to arrange for insurance for a small team, since the benefits brokers aren't interested. Any employment contract with employees needs to be locally compliant as well, which is another factor you need to consider. However, if you're based in the U.S., you also want to make sure that your intellectual property (IP) is owned by the U.S. parent company, whatever the relationship is with the international office, even though your employee is physically working for you from a different country. IP ownership needs to be stipulated in the employment contract, and also through intercompany service agreements that detail ownership rights and how each entity can use intellectual property belonging to the group.

In addition, if you're a U.S. company, you also need to be certain that your international office is following U.S. law, which includes ensuring that you're not accidentally paying anyone on a terrorist watch list, for example. That's important since the penalty is having your business bank account shut down and being fined US$10,000 a day until the situation is corrected. Imagine what that means if you're operating in 18 countries—the math gets exorbitant on Day 1, not to mention the operational risk. Any misstep gets costly, quickly. Missteps such as forgetting to lock down IP ownership in employment agreements with local employees, and in compliance with local labor law, can ultimately cost a company the company itself, if not discovered until the time of a long-sought exit.

ZOOM

Before going public in April 2019, about 20 percent of Zoom's video meeting business was outside the U.S. Total revenue had hit US$300 million, with around US$60 million generated from international markets. Fast forward two and a half years, in the first quarter of fiscal year 2021, Zoom had about 34 percent of its business originate in APAC and EMEA; the equivalent of about US$331 million. Today, toward the end of fiscal 2021, Zoom's non-U.S. revenue is projected to hit US$1 billion.

In one year, from 2020 to 2021, Zoom grew by about 3,000 employees, many of whom are located outside the U.S. That is part of the company's strategy to build a team of world-class Zoomies to support its clients around the world.

Strong teams are now in place around the globe, thanks to Globalization Partners' help. Japan's team continues to grow while generating significant revenue. Europe and EMEA contribute a sizeable portion of the region's sales. The UK, France, Germany, the Middle East, Eastern Europe, and Africa are all expanding. In Latin America, Zoom has expanded in Brazil and Mexico and is also serving Argentina and Chile.

But Zoom is just getting started. Many of the trends that came to the fore during the pandemic were already on the company's radar. The rise of the remote worker, the gig economy, and distance learning were already emerging. And how generations converging in the workplace are changing how work is done, with digital native Gen Z and Millennials leading the way, had appeared as a new challenge. The need for productivity also fueled the use of video, especially in cities where traffic eats into the workday. These issues were converging, but the pandemic pushed people to make a shift.

On the education front, almost overnight, learning had to be relocated from the classroom to the kitchen table at the same time business moved from the boardroom to the living room. These transitions pushed people to rethink how they worked or educated themselves, and how they socialized. This awakening is a whole new way of being and an amazing opportunity that Zoom is both humbled and excited to be part of—Zoom wants to be everywhere its customers are.

Globalization Partners has played a critical role in Zoom's expansion strategy. The company is entering a number of markets quickly and can rely on Globalization Partners' agility and speed to do that. Having a great employee experience is important at Zoom, starting with how employees are onboarded. They are full-time Zoomies whether they live in Europe, Latin America, or Asia-Pacific. In the past few months, there have been decisions that required the company to turn on a dime, entering a country quickly and hiring employees on the ground there. Globalization Partners gave Zoom the support and flexibility it needed to be successful. And in more complicated regions, such as the Middle East, Globalization Partners has provided the guidance and nimbleness Zoom needed.

Zoom as a company is focused on delivering happiness to its employees, its customers, and the community. Its talented team faced the challenges of the pandemic and rose to the occasion to make it possible for people to remain connected. It continues to add team members, and the need for video connections shows no sign of slowing.

RECENT GLOBALIZATION CATALYSTS

In spite of the complexities of expanding internationally the old-fashioned way, most companies soldiered on in search of the many benefits of a global workforce. Initially, the prospect of lower labor costs drove much of the growth, which is why massive call centers sprang up in countries like India, China, and the Philippines; labor costs were much, much lower than in the U.S. But today there are many other factors at play that are driving up an interest in building global teams, namely:

- **Talent gap:** A lack of qualified talent to fill key technology roles in developed countries has effectively forced companies to seek out workers in other localities. There are too few engineers in the U.S., and economists have suggested a need for 1 million more STEM professionals by 2025 than the U.S. is currently producing, which is pushing recruitment efforts outside North America.[14] There are software companies growing at a rapid pace globally, and yet, there is a shortage of specialized knowledge. As a result, organizations are recruiting in Ireland, Poland, or Romania to get the skills they need. Beyond that, companies have realized that they can hire excellent lower-cost talent outside their HQ locations and are maximizing their opportunity.

- **Revenue growth:** Hiring a sales team based in Europe to tackle the European market is much more effective than trying to do so from the U.S. It's also easier than expected, with the right talent. Apply that same strategy in every region in the world, and your potential as a business is exponential compared to a domestic-only mindset.

- **Restrictive immigration policies:** Companies in high-growth industries used to import talent, sponsoring work permits for high-value employees. However, as part of protectionist labor policies, many developed countries have started significantly restricting the ability of companies to import talent. The companies are hiring the same talent that they need, but only by letting employees work remotely from their home countries rather than trying to get through the arduous H-1B visa (or equivalent) process.

- **Mindset shift:** As a society, the concept of remote work has become much more of an accepted practice—the standard rather than the exception, especially as the pandemic hit and drove workers home in order to stay healthy. Generational shifts in the workplace and the rising demand for more flexible work options are also impacting this growth. A highly talented futurist in a developing country might want to live and work on the beach or in the mountains—and most companies will enable that flexibility for highly specialized talent. Especially in a post-pandemic world, competitive employers have to be flexible to retain the world's best talent.

- **Technology advances:** New software tools that enable remote communication, such as Zoom for videoconferencing and Slack and Trello for remote team project management, have reduced the feeling of disconnectedness and lack of work oversight managers have long feared. Beyond that, studies such as those done by Microsoft and McKinsey in mid-2020 have demonstrated that workers are indeed as effective or more effective working from home than most executives ever imagined possible.

The global Employer of Record industry (outlined later in this chapter) and advances in technology, combined with the culture shift triggered by the pandemic, have flung the doors to global remote work wide open. The world is at your doorstep, and now is the time to go global.

NEURALA

Neurala is a Boston-based pioneer in vision AI software, on a mission to make AI more applicable and useful in real-world applications. Specifically, the company helps industrial companies improve their quality-inspection process through technology that dramatically reduces the time, cost, and skills required to build and maintain production-quality, custom vision AI solutions.

Founded in 2006 by Heather Ames, Max Versace, and Anatoli Gorchet, Neurala invented Lifelong-DNN™ (L-DNN) technology, which lowers the data requirements for AI model development and enables continuous learning in the cloud or at the edge. The company currently has approximately 40 employees, some of whom work from the office as needed and the rest working 100 percent remotely.

The founders always knew that a global mindset would be essential for the company's growth.

Expansion began in 2018 through work with a large telecom company based out of China. Since then, Neurala pivoted the focus of its business to the manufacturing industry, seeing a big opportunity for its technology in that space. Having a global reach will continue to be important.

Its leaders tried to be strategic and intentional about the locations they targeted for business, considering regions outside of North America, like APAC and EMEA, which have a strong manufacturing presence. Areas where Neurala has already had success include Europe—Italy, in particular. The fact that CEO and co-founder Versace was born and raised in Italy has helped the business establish a strong foothold there. With his background and ties to the region, Neurala has been able to make strong connections with manufacturers there that continue to present opportunities for partnership and growth.

That said, the pandemic complicated things, making travel challenging. In-person, on-the-ground meetings with manufacturers are so much more effective for Neurala's sales process, since what the company offers is so visual, but, as with most other companies, the pandemic forced a switch to Zoom meetings.

The pandemic did foster a new company culture, spreading a greater sense of understanding and camaraderie throughout the organization. With everyone on video calls all day long, there have been a number of shared funny moments when kids have interrupted calls.

That's become the norm. It shows everyone a different side of your team, and employees have come to appreciate that as a silver lining.

Pandemic aside, the company still wants to be able to give manufacturers the guidance and knowledge needed to succeed. So, in the fall of 2020, the company launched its Neurala VIA Authorized Partner program. This global network of integrators and distributors is able to leverage a vast range of expertise to help manufacturers adopt automation and implement Industry 4.0 initiatives. After Neurala spoke with end users and partners, it was evident that partnering with local experts would be the key.

Thanks to tools like Zoom and Microsoft Teams, nearly everyone is comfortable communicating via video. That's also led to increased comfort with hiring people through video interviews, as opposed to in-person meetings. That process has become the norm now, whether the candidate is in the U.S. or on another continent.

Neurala has recognized the importance of having local partners and experts on the ground and plans to continue expanding its own footprint outside of its HQ in North America. It typically leverages Globalization Partners' platform to hire employees outside the U.S., enabling the executive team to remain nimble while still garnering the highly valued talent it needs.

Cost of living ↓

San Francisco
rents dropped
↓ 35%

Boston rents
dropped
↓ 18%

© Globalization Partners, Inc.

REMOTE WORK GOES MAINSTREAM

The biggest enabler of the recent international push has been the growing acceptance of remote work. With a declining reliance on face-to-face, in-person meetings and an increasing comfort level with supervision from afar, location has become less essential, or perhaps less relevant. An October 2020 Gallup poll reported that 33 percent of American workers claim they "always" work remotely, which is down 18 percent from the start of the pandemic in April 2020, when 51 percent of workers in the U.S. indicated they always worked remotely.

However, the percentage of workers who "sometimes" work remotely has risen, from 18 percent to 25 percent.[15] Together, those two figures indicate that the majority of U.S. workers, 58 percent, worked remotely at least part of the time as of late 2020.

THE GLOBAL EMPLOYER OF RECORD MODEL: THE NEW WAY COMPANIES GO GLOBAL

Although, historically, setting up a new operation in another country has been complex and involved, there is a new way that offers organizations a shortcut to doing business internationally: the Employer of Record model, which I launched almost 10 years ago, vastly improves the quality and size of the talent pool companies can tap.

An Employer of Record acts as the official employer of your workers and relieves hiring organizations of doing the heavy lifting of setting up and staffing a location in another country. Since we know that the process of setting up a branch office registration in another country can take up to a year, that lag time can dampen corporate enthusiasm, as well as growth. With an in-country Employer of Record, you leapfrog over those infrastructure requirements and can add international employees in a couple of hours instead of months. We believe that's a key reason companies are flooding the market to hire global talent faster than ever.

The industry's closest ancestor may be the temporary staffing agency, but an Employer of Record is unique: it is the sole direct legal employer of individuals hand-selected by its customers. Essentially, customers identify the talent, and the Employer of Record puts their team members on an already-existing local payroll and benefits plan. As the contracting company, you're outsourcing your international legal, HR, and finance functions, so a competent Employer of Record should have built the necessary global legal infrastructure and software. It should have HR team members around the globe to advise customers on managing their workforce as well as an in-house legal team—especially useful in countries where terminating an employee is extremely difficult. It should be compliant with EU data privacy regulations and have carefully thought through both the local and global issues companies face in cross-border business. It should also regularly test (and certify) its software for the cybersecurity necessary to employ thousands of people globally.

As an expert on local rules and regulations, the Employer of Record should be responsible for ensuring that all local laws are being followed during the hiring process, that benefits offered are legal and appropriate for the region, and that the onboarding process complies with local regulations. In most jurisdictions, the customer oversees the hiring decisions and determines day-to-day activities. (Slight variations exist where local regulations require it, but in general, individuals hired by the Employer of Record provide services to the customer in the country of service.) Keep in mind that this is a new industry, and not all options are created equal. A high-quality Employer of Record is always available to talk through challenges customers may face to ensure that the solution is legal and fair. If an Employer of Record does all that, and maintains world-class compliance standards, the customers can easily access talent without having to navigate the complexities of global business before even getting started.

HOW TO STRUCTURE YOUR TEAM

Now that remote work is possible almost across the board, more companies are exploring the ramifications of that new capability. We're seeing many companies choose lower-cost international locations when they can—for example, Boston-headquartered companies are looking at St. Louis, and San Francisco has seen an exodus to Texas. North American-headquartered companies also hire in Toronto, Mexico, and Central/South America. Typically, locations that companies choose have a few things in common:

- They are in a similar time zone as the customer(s)

- Local residents are polished English speakers

- There are pods, or groups, of highly skilled talent available

- In particular, there is abundant tech talent available

- The salespeople are culturally and geographically near the buyer

Geographic and time zone proximity makes human resource management easier, and the availability of talent makes high performance possible, but familiarity with or similarities to the end user/buyer may be among the most important factors, especially in sales. Workers who are able to easily connect with buyers because of similar values, mannerisms, and personalities can achieve sales results that meet or exceed workers in the home country.

> *When you're engaging an Employer of Record, you're essentially outsourcing your international legal, HR, and finance infrastructure—focusing on quality is critical. This is a new industry, and all options are not created equal.*

UDEMY

Udemy is the leading destination for online learning. At the onset of the pandemic lockdown in 2020, Udemy saw a large spike on its learning platform. People were losing their jobs and decided to take the opportunity to learn and upskill so that when they went back to work, they would be ready and positioned for better opportunities.

Interestingly Udemy also saw companies double down on providing access to the platform as a benefit for their employees. Corporations realized they were entering a new paradigm of work and there was a need to provide education and upskilling in a remote-first environment. Udemy is made for that. While demand surged for its online courses, Udemy had already been taking steps to expand geographically at scale. The company takes a three-pronged approach to growing its teams, focusing on a great experience for its customers, business stakeholders, and employees.

It has recruiting teams located in primary hubs—San Francisco, Dublin, Turkey, and Australia—that partner with local leadership to help scale the company globally. Udemy is currently hiring around the globe across many functions, including technology, systems support, accounting, marketing, sales, and customer success. From a logistics perspective, Udemy has found that in many cases, the cost and time to establish entities in every country where the company needed employees was prohibitive and did not scale at the pace required, so it has relied on Globalization Partners to help employ people outside of its primary global hubs more efficiently.

In addition, the goal of providing both a great candidate and employee experience is a priority. While Udemy has learned the art of structuring a personalized interview process and hiring over Zoom during the pandemic, it has relied on Globalization Partners to help *execute at the contractual level and ensure that employees have benefits and a knowledgeable human resources partner wherever they may live or work. As Udemy looks forward, it expects to continue to hire on a global scale. As of August 2021, Globalization Partners has already helped Udemy add 100 employees worldwide.*

BUYER BEWARE

The global Employer of Record industry is a high-growth opportunity that is mostly unregulated. There are many players in the industry that have been built on a shoestring, with policies and procedures that may or may not be sufficient. When evaluating global Employer of Record providers, inquire about the following:

- Who founded the company?

- Who are their investors?

- How long have they been in business?

- Do they have their own entities in place, or are they relying on local mom-and-pop shops in foreign countries to be the actual employers?

- Was their infrastructure built by a world-class team, taking local and global legal requirements into account?

- Are their claims realistic?

- Do they have technology platforms to manage details like employee data, payroll, PTO tracking, expenses, and employment contracts?

- Is their software tested and certified for cybersecurity compliance?

- Do they have dedicated teams available to answer questions when they come up? Where are those teams located?

- Can they offer supplemental benefit group plans?

- Do they manage data in accordance with EU data privacy standards or local in-country standards?

- How are fees and markups expressed on invoices?

- What percent of their workforce is dedicated to human resources, legal, and customer support?

- Do they have in-house HR specialists located in local markets?

- How easy is it to get accurate HR advice from them, and how long does it take? When creating a global employee experience, this is critical.

- How do they follow data security requirements?

- What is their payroll accuracy level?

- How is their financial health?

- What are their long-term plans?

- What are their reputations for customer service?

What you want to hear in response to these questions is honesty and transparency. Will you be charged for every question or phone call you make, for example? How quickly is the company expanding globally, and what's their track record? Are you confident in their expertise and ability to accurately advise your company when issues arise? You need to feel confident that your global employment partner is equipped to guide and protect you in countries where you've never done business before, and ensure you're operating above the law. When you're outsourcing your global employment infrastructure, quality is critical.

ADDITIONAL RESOURCES

You'll find useful resources related to expanding your company internationally at globaltalentunleashed.com/chapter-1

CHAPTER 2

*Hiring Global Talent
Is the Norm of the Future*

Fear of hiring an employee who isn't on-site, or even local, is the biggest obstacle fast-growth companies have to overcome in order to build the team of their dreams. In order to completely avoid the whole situation, companies find workarounds that suffice on a temporary basis, but ultimately have significant disadvantages.

One of Globalization Partners' customers is a U.S.-based software company with clients across the country and in Europe and Asia. In the mid-2000s, the company was in demand and would routinely decline non-U.S. business opportunities that would have required putting an employee in place in another country. Or, they might have accepted a new business opportunity in Europe and then serviced it from the U.S., flying key executives to meetings "across the pond." They would fly someone from the U.S. headquarters to Paris for a meeting one day and to London later in the week, rather than hiring someone close to the customer. It was easier for the company to manage their local employee that way, they had convinced themselves, and they didn't want to deal with hiring internationally.

Over time, however, as the relationship with the customer in France grew, the CEO became increasingly pressured to hire someone closer to the customer to service that relationship.

"Look, we're in Europe. We'd really rather have a European customer service support person than someone based in the U.S. Have you considered having our support based here?" the customer asked.

In fact, they had considered and routinely talked themselves out of it. In this particular case, the idea of having an employee so far away who was supposed to be working on behalf of the company, sight unseen, was worrisome. They were also unfamiliar with how to even start the process of finding a skilled employee on a different continent. They didn't know what the rules and regulations were regarding hiring and employment in Europe, but they knew the employment laws wouldn't be anything like those they knew in the U.S. Hiring in France, in particular, was intimidating—France is notorious for HR horror stories, and is considered more worker-friendly than perhaps any other part of the world.

Once hired, how would the company train this new hire from afar, they wondered, having never done it before? The list of reasons not to even attempt an international hire seemed to get longer every time the executive team had the discussion.

Yet eventually, the customer prevailed and the company, with much trepidation, finally proceeded to find and hire a single employee on the ground in France. They hired the employee via Globalization Partners' global employment platform, transferring the responsibility for the notorious French labor laws management to our capable team.

You know what happened? First of all, the company's existing business in Europe flourished. Having just one local person there, in a local office, increased customer satisfaction tremendously, and second, it attracted more work from the region almost instantly. Suddenly, having someone there who spoke the local language, who was in the same time zone, who was able to problem solve on the spot was extremely attractive to other organizations in the area that had been reluctant to hire a U.S. company with no local representation. It turned out that hiring the employee in France was not a nightmare—it was a godsend.

Having someone in France also made management's job so much easier, they were surprised to find. No more flying people to international meetings or trying to understand what the customer really needed from thousands of miles away and in early morning phone calls. A local employee fundamentally simplified the customer relationship and reduced the work to be done and the strain on its U.S. team.

That first successful hire quickly led to more hires throughout the European region, which only fueled more demand for its services. Within a few short years, its European clientele accounted for 40 percent of the business's total revenue.

Once the company was able to justify the setup work that might be required to find, hire, train, and set a new employee up in an office in Europe, the floodgates opened as far as business was concerned. In the back of their minds, management had known this was a possibility. It was just the fear of how much work would actually be involved that had been the stumbling block. Having never hired anyone abroad before, they had only assumptions and fears to rely on rather than experience or facts.

Today that company has expanded not only throughout Europe but also in Asia. They've even hired a few engineers in Uruguay and Mexico. The CEO regularly credits the ease of being able to hire people via our platform, and taking that initial first step, as critical to the company's resounding success.

GETTING OUT OF YOUR OWN WAY

That fear of the unknown, of what can go wrong if you make a poor hire, even held Globalization Partners back a little early on. We were setting up our Mexico City office and our head of operations and legal counsel were working together to get everything in place, but it was a little challenging because much of the business in Mexico City gets done in person; it's very relationship-oriented, and building relationships is key to success. We knew we had to have someone there heading up our office, so our team went down to interview candidates. These were people who were going to be responsible for starting our Mexico City operations. It was a big job, and there was a lot on the line if they made a poor choice. We kept thinking we would get it set up and then hire the local talent. Wouldn't you think by then we would be following our own advice? Unfortunately, for some reason, we had held back.

While there, our team members interviewed a candidate who seemed great. We hired him. Communication in Mexico is not quite as direct as the U.S., so even as we handed all the work off to him, our management team was nervous about the reality of the situation. Could he really do all that he said he could? Was he really as capable as he seemed?

In a word, yes, he really could, we quickly learned.

Within days of starting, our new hire joined important legal and tax meetings in Mexico as the company's representative, identifying, addressing, and fixing problems as soon as they came up. He was exactly who we needed at that moment, and he made it possible for Globalization Partners to grow so much faster, thanks to his work ethic, intelligence, and ability to forge and maintain relationships. We called him our unicorn, because, at the time, we couldn't imagine a more perfect person for the job we needed done.

We now have well over 100 employees in Mexico working on our internal operations, as well as hundreds who provide services to our customers. It has become a major operational hub for our company.

Our team in Mexico is exceptionally talented, all English-speaking, and our expansion plans there took off because we made that brave step of hiring our first in-house person locally to handle our necessary Mexico business.

Getting Started: Finding Talent

Finding workers has been a major obstacle for many organizations to overcome. Even the idea of putting up a job posting in a country halfway around the world has made companies pause and confirm whether this is really what they want to do. The reality, however, is that the employee recruitment process is much the same across the world, from Poland to Portugal to the U.S.

The first step is drafting a clear description of the job, which probably exists already if you've previously had someone in that role, and the second is posting it on job boards with an international audience. LinkedIn is the most commonly used platform by our customers for international hires. There are also more country-focused sites as well. Beyond that, local recruiters can, of course, work their charm, and are often a valuable investment. In all, though, it's easier than you think, and many of our customers are surprised how quickly they're able to recruit talent the same way they do in the U.S.—through LinkedIn.

THE ADVANTAGE OF FACE-TO-FACE COMMUNICATION

Although many companies fear the inability to monitor workers in person, there is a significant advantage to having customer-facing employees in another country. That close customer proximity, regardless of distance to the home office, reduces the incidence of miscommunication and misunderstanding that can occur through other means of communication, such as email, text, and even phone.

For example, in some Asian countries, there is a strong preference for use of the phone or video call to communicate, more so than email, especially if there's anything nuanced to discuss—if you have a question or concern, they generally prefer a phone call. In North Asia, face-to-face meetings are preferred, as these are high-context countries, where nonverbal communications are absolutely critical to workplace interactions. Americans rely heavily on email, but the truth is that, in Asia, it takes so much longer to type out information in English in an email that they would much prefer to receive a phone call in their native language. Like in most countries, this is much more efficient, and it reduces the chance of miscommunication.

But there are many situations that can be misconstrued, even by phone. For example, while in some Asian countries the lack of response to a question could indicate acceptance, it is common knowledge that in Japan silence might mean "no." Residents of some countries are culturally taught never to use the word "no." Coming right out and stating it so boldly is considered rude, so they dance around the answer, and not all Americans pick up on it, especially from afar. In fact, Americans hate it when someone doesn't respond—it's a surefire way of setting their hair on fire, and much worse (to us) than hearing "no."

There's a funny scenario I share that underscores some of the issues that come up frequently. Picture an American executive who calls a Japanese accountant to problem solve a compliance situation.

"Can we handle this situation this way?" the American asks the Japanese manager.

"It would be difficult," replies the accountant.

The American interprets this as implying that the solution may be more expensive than expected or will take more time to get done. So the American asks, "Oh, okay, well, what will it take to get it done?"

The accountant repeats, "It's very difficult."

The American thinks the Japanese accountant is underscoring, literally, the degree of difficulty to continue with that course of action. In the American mindset, that probably means some time and a large invoice can be expected. So the American executive asks, "Okay, well, just tell me what it will take to get it done and we can then decide if we want to take that approach."

They hear nothing but silence from the other end.

The American gets increasingly frustrated that someone is completely ignoring their question, when the Japanese feels they have said "it's impossible" twice and doesn't understand why the customer keeps pushing on that. Their response has been clear and consistent—it can't be done.

Not disappointing anyone is another reason some business professionals in various cultures avoid the word "no" at all costs. Of course, it can cause problems, often large, when you don't realize you're being told "no." Americans expect to be told "no" directly and don't always pick up on the nuances.

My chief operating officer, Debbie Millin, was working with a former employer on a major project undertaken by a team in India. She would get on phone calls to discuss the status of the project and everyone else would be really quiet, she recalled. No one would ever say that the work couldn't be done or wouldn't be done, but she wouldn't get much in the way of a status report when she asked for it.

The night before the deadline, Debbie received a call from a nervous manager to tell her there was no way the project would be delivered any time soon.

"Why didn't you tell me that several weeks ago?" she wanted to know. And the response was that they didn't want to disappoint her with the truth and avoided the topic.

Where Americans are direct in spoken communication once we're familiar with a colleague or acquaintance, many cultures in Asia tend to be indirect even after rapport is built. The responsibility shifts from the communicator to share information to the listener to pick up what is being conveyed between the lines. Although you might never hear the word "no" spoken, you may get recommendations for other service providers, because they can't do what you need, or you may hear that the person you've asked needs to check with their manager. Subtly, you're being told "no," and you have to listen to the implied message to understand that. This is thanks to generations of social cohesion and alignment. If we must generalize about Asian societies, the largest difference from the West is their commitment to academic excellence and social solidarity as well as synergy between state and society. This is felt in the muted assertiveness that other cultures often detect.

Not disappointing anyone is another reason some business professionals in various cultures avoid the word "no" at all costs. Of course, it can cause problems, often large, when you don't realize you're being told "no."

Similarly, in an effort to be polite, some Asian businesspeople will nod their heads to convey that they've heard you. "I understand the words you're saying," is what that head nod means, yet Americans interpret that nod to mean, "Yes, I agree. We're in alignment. We're all set."

The nodder is really only saying, "Interesting idea!"

That's one challenge of trying to manage someone, or a customer relationship, from another continent or time zone. These nuanced situations come up that are mystifying and that could have been avoided or resolved much more quickly if there had been someone working in that office or who could show up in person to get something done. It both eases and solidifies customer relationships to have someone close by.

As a side note, we should all be grateful for video teleconferencing technology. It's so much easier to read body language—and, indeed, understand a foreign language—when you can see the person you're speaking with. We recommend using video telecommunications as much as possible when working as a global remote team.

PUSHING PAST THE FEAR
OF HIRING OFF-SITE WORKERS

Are there pitfalls associated with hiring workers remotely? Absolutely. And they hold true whether your next hire is located on the other side of the state, the country, or the world. No matter where your next hire resides, your recruitment, hiring, and onboarding process should remain the same. That means carefully reviewing all of the résumés candidates submit, checking their references, and interviewing them by video—often conducting multiple interviews, depending on the role and level of responsibility—to get to a point where you feel confident of your assessment of the candidate's abilities.

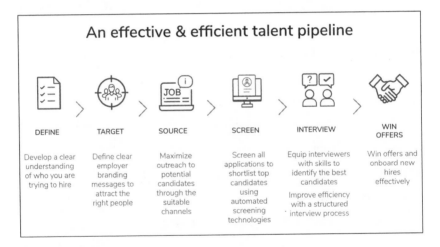

An effective & efficient talent pipeline

DEFINE	TARGET	SOURCE	SCREEN	INTERVIEW	WIN OFFERS
Develop a clear understanding of who you are trying to hire	Define clear employer branding messages to attract the right people	Maximize outreach to potential candidates through the suitable channels	Screen all applications to shortlist top candidates using automated screening technologies	Equip interviewers with skills to identify the best candidates Improve efficiency with a structured interview process	Win offers and onboard new hires effectively

That's a fairly standard and successful process for most organizations. At Globalization Partners, we have witnessed 90 percent of those hired using that process, coupled with a strong onboarding, typically stick around for at least a year, whereas 10 percent of new employees are terminated within the first six to 12 months. That figure holds steady whether we're talking about hiring in the U.S. or anywhere else in the world.

The vast majority of those who leave or are let go after only a few months do so because of a problem with the onboarding process. If a company doesn't have an effective onboarding process, new employees will not understand or feel part of the organization's culture. Feeling left out or abandoned is not conducive to retaining employees, remote or not.

The key with onboarding is that you should invest the same amount of time training a new employee regardless of their location. That is, employees who are working locally should receive the same quality of training and amount of attention as someone who is being trained remotely in Dublin, Des Moines, or Denmark.

Globalization Partners uses a software kit called Lessonly for automated training as part of its onboarding process, though there are certainly several software options available. Lessonly enabled us to create internal training materials for our team so that team members can self-educate and test themselves long before they interface with our customers. We also have created certification tools for mastery of knowledge related to new countries and software, which enables employees to demonstrate they have the skills needed for promotions. Investing in digital learning tools is the only way to build a global remote team at scale without investing repetitive man-hours in training people. Training software also enables team members to learn at their own pace and in their own time zones.

ALWAYS HAVE A WAY OUT

At-will employment is an almost uniquely American way of doing business; one of the bigger issues that most American companies get into is not realizing that terminating an employee is much more challenging (and expensive) outside the U.S. The best way to navigate this is by carefully considering each new hire and implementing a probation period when necessary.

During those initial weeks and months, when you're wondering if your latest hire is going to work out, keep in mind that there can almost always be a probationary period written into all global employment contracts. That probationary, or trial, period lasting anywhere from 30 to 90 days, depending on the laws in the country, is an opportunity for both parties to try out the relationship. If it becomes clear that it isn't going to work, the probationary status of that employment relationship makes it fairly easy to end it as painlessly as possible. Globalization Partners does recommend exercising all termination with care for the worker, whether long-term or short-term, but we've also found it's always better to decide sooner rather than later if someone isn't going to work out—ideally, within the probationary period.

This probationary period should help allay many of the fears you may have about hiring someone in another country. Thanks to the probationary period included as part of a locally compliant employment contract, letting go of employees who are not going to work out is fairly straightforward if it's done during the trial period. Then, it doesn't matter if those employees didn't work out because they overstated their qualifications, misunderstood what their role would be, were more introvert than extrovert for the sales position they accepted, were not working during the company's established work hours, or because they were rude to fellow employees. The probationary period is a way out if you begin to rethink the choice of your new hire.

The good news is that even when an employee doesn't work out, you've still gained more than you've lost because you've learned something about hiring people in that area. And since your local office is already operational, finding, hiring, and onboarding a new person will take much less time in the future.

REMOTION

Remotion is a video workspace for remote teams with a distributed workforce of approximately 10 employees based in San Francisco, Chicago, New York City, the UK, Australia, Canada, and Uruguay. The company has been hiring internationally from the start, including its first employee, who was in Uruguay. At the time, time zone overlap was critical.

Following hiring success in Uruguay, Remotion had success with finding high-performance talent in the U.S., which also provided time zone overlap for effective collaboration. Strong writing and communication skills were also important, which is why the company continued hiring initially in countries with strong English-language education. That led to subsequent hires in Canada, the UK, and Latin America.

Having the ability to hire anywhere is a core company value— the expanded candidate pool means Remotion can hire the strongest candidates available no matter where they are, allowing the company to hire top candidates faster. In addition, bringing in global talent gives it a broader perspective and allows it to better support its global user base.

Since Remotion has worked 100 percent remotely for years, it recognized that having a strong infrastructure for hiring anywhere is crucial for having a stable team. Because employees' rights are respected and they're treated as local employees and in accordance with the law in each country where they work, they are happy. Globalization Partners' global employment platform enables Remotion to truly hire and retain the best talent they can find, anywhere in the world, quickly and easily.

THE DEMOCRATIZATION OF THE WORKFORCE

The willingness of U.S. companies to consider hiring workers who don't operate out of U.S.-based offices and facilities is the result of a workplace evolution that has been accelerated by the pandemic. Organizations that may have wondered if remote work is an option they should offer employees, due to rising demand, learned quickly in 2020 that many professional jobs can certainly be done remotely. Many companies realized that there was truly nothing standing in the way of them allowing white-collar workers to work from home, or a space other than their office. Many companies intend to continue to offer employees the option to work remotely post-pandemic, including Facebook and Twitter, which made remote work a permanent option for its employees.

With employees able to work anywhere, growing companies are now drastically expanding their hiring pool. Rather than hiring employees within a certain radius of headquarters or offices, companies can hire from anywhere in the world they can find talented people. From the employee perspective, the news is also good, as new opportunities emerge. However, where they used to compete with candidates within a 50- to 100-mile radius of an organization's offices, that competition has now expanded to include anyone in the world.

Where job opportunities have expanded exponentially, real estate shifts are occurring, too. Employees who formerly had to live in high-cost-of-living areas to maintain their high-paying jobs now have the freedom to live anywhere. Some San Francisco residents, for example, recognized this new opportunity and decided to relocate to Montana, where housing is much more affordable and spacious. This drove up the value of real estate in Montana by 20 percent fairly quickly.[16] Once one employee is in a new location, it also drives future hires to that area. This move toward remote work has incredible potential to heal some of the divisions in our society.

By spreading jobs out more evenly across the U.S., there will be less income inequality. There will be higher paying jobs found in places outside major cities, which is beneficial to workers in the smaller towns and cities that suffered when manufacturing jobs disappeared. A broader range of opportunities with a broader range of incomes will become the norm, sparked by rising acceptance of remote work as a standard business practice.

At the same time, as higher-paying jobs become more plentiful in smaller cities, lower-paying jobs will also continue to be created internationally, in lower-cost areas. We've already seen this happening, and it will continue. In turn, increasing opportunities in other parts of the world will accelerate the rise of the middle class in other countries.

Extreme poverty worldwide has been on the decline for the last 20 years or so, according to World Vision, in part due to the rise of a global workforce.[17] According to Bill Gates, around the year 2000, 30 percent of the world's inhabitants were living in extreme poverty—no running water, electricity, or food stability. Today, that number is closer to 10 percent. We've made great strides. It's a UN Millennium Development Goal to end extreme poverty by 2030,[18] and we are thrilled and delighted to think that Globalization Partners will play even a small role in contributing to that.

The impact of remote work on society as a whole has been huge, and the transformation is still underway. For companies looking to expand their geographic footprint, the ability for employees to work from anywhere has virtually eliminated any previous hiring barriers. The opportunities are only going to increase, and the impact of harnessing the greatness of everyone, everywhere, is incredibly exciting—for all of us.

ADDITIONAL RESOURCES

You'll find useful resources related to hiring at globaltalentunleashed.com/chapter-2

PART II

Focus on Your Hiring Strategy for Global Success

The process of expanding into new geographic regions begins with a plan—where are you going, why are you going, and who do you need to hire to accomplish your goals? And, just as important—where are those people located?

Rather than starting by posting job openings worldwide, a more methodical approach to planning your global footprint first can help reduce your workload and provide focus for where you can find the talent you need to accomplish your goals.

CHAPTER 3

The Path to Finding Global Talent

Although global expansion is a business strategy for growth, at its core it is a human resource plan. To be able to successfully grow into new geographic territories, if you plan on hiring an entire team in any location, you need talented leaders in place first. You can't expect to move into an area by hiring entry-level workers—without someone to lead them, you're unlikely to be successful. Of course, if you're just hiring one or two people in a country and the person you're hiring is okay working as the sole contributor in that location, hire away. Many of our customers are indeed doing that and, thus, leveraging our platform to hire "anyone, anywhere" who is most qualified to get the job done. We applaud this approach and love the democratization of opportunity it offers people.

There is no one single path to global expansion, no one "right way." Your own company's approach to growth will depend on several factors, starting with the industry in which you operate. Your industry and the market you serve will determine the type of talent you need, which then points you in the direction of the talent pools you'll want to tap into and in which order.

For example, a software as a service (SaaS) company might need to get engineering teams in place in major markets first, with the priority being hiring the best talent for the best value. Whereas a publishing venture might first need legal teams and content creators in its major markets, and an e-commerce site might need merchandise buyers and logistics pros before other professionals.

The type of talent you need, and the global talent pools you may zero in on, will depend primarily on your intentions, your industry, and your customer base.

IF YOUR GOAL IS TO BUILD GLOBAL REVENUE, HIRE EXECUTIVE LEADERSHIP IN-REGION FIRST

No matter your industry, one of the first hires you should consider making when entering a new geographic region with the intention of building a sales team is executive talent. That usually means a vice president (VP) of sales in a key strategic location and a back office to support marketing efforts and customers. The back-office team may potentially be located in a lower-cost jurisdiction in the same time zone, with lots of talent.

Of course, you're more likely to find strategic sales leaders in major cities, where big companies are located—cities like San Francisco, Boston, London, Dublin, Hong Kong, Berlin, or Singapore. Think about which companies are likely to employ your perfect next hire and where those companies are currently headquartered. For example, do you need a head of sales to build and run your partners team for a tech company in Europe? Local recruiters might suggest you look for your VP of sales in London or Berlin. Fashion marketing gurus might look in Paris. List the companies that employ the types of talent you need and then identify their headquarters and global hubs. Most likely, those hubs are in the world's largest cities.

That's where you need to start your own search, when it comes to finding and hiring your key executive talent and deal closers.

At Globalization Partners, when we begin the recruitment process for someone who is at the VP level or above, we're primarily looking for people who have experience in world-class companies. That's the first prerequisite. Those companies often include organizations like LinkedIn, Google, Amazon, or Wayfair, just to name a few. So, we begin our search within cities where those types of companies are located—meaning tech hubs, or cities that are home to large tech companies.

One benefit of starting with senior talent is that they can quickly and effectively build a team beneath them. They have the network and the chops to have "been there, done that," and they can do it again.

In the early days of Globalization Partners, my goal was to build an executive team in Boston because I lived there. There was so much travel required for the business that I didn't want to have to do any additional traveling to meet with my C-suite and VP-level hires. Finding top talent was easier because they were likely already in Boston working for another employer, since Boston is home to a number of corporate giants. Bringing them on board was easier because we were confident we could find local talent; relocation wouldn't be necessary.

This approach has since become obsolete; I moved to California, and my C-suite is closely knit enough that we collaborate like champions, mostly via Zoom. We meet in person regularly, and I've started hiring more Bay Area-based VPs to align with our typical U.S. customer profile. Beyond that, we have executives in Singapore, London, and, by now, every corner of the globe. Individuals no longer have to be somewhere specific, as is the case in many industries. Yet, it does remain critical for executives to come with world-class experience and a strong network. We still find that level of talent largely clustered around large cities, or at least with a recent work history centered around those locations.

COLD CHAIN TECHNOLOGIES

Founded in 1967, Cold Chain Technologies (CCT) is a leading provider of reusable and single-use thermal packaging solutions, supporting the distribution of temperature-sensitive life science shipments around the globe. Through the design, manufacture, and supply of innovative shipping systems, as well as customized delivery solutions, the company helps protect the integrity of temperature-sensitive, healthcare-related products worldwide. In 2020, CCT also acquired DuPont's Tyvek cargo covers business, which serves the global life science industry.

With 50 years of experience in the cold chain industry, CCT understands its logistics, applications, demands, and extremes, and has its own R&D, manufacturing, sales, distribution, and service functions. Its workforce consists of both permanent employees and a large contract team, which enables the company to effectively react to surge activity related to vaccine deployment.

Since its life science partners have global operations, they look to CCT to provide its solutions and services globally, too. That demand is driving CCT's geographic expansion plans.

The company's global expansion began many years ago through a partner in the Netherlands who helped the company access the

EMEA market. CCT's operations in Singapore serve as a hub for Asia, and its offices in Panama and São Paulo serve Latin America.

The thermal packaging market is large, and by expanding into parts of EMEA, LATAM, and APAC, the company can now sell there. This expansion has helped further accelerate the growth trajectory of CCT. Its presence in Europe—one of its most successful sales regions— which is a mature market for healthcare and medical products, is currently self-sustaining with plans for additional growth underway.

As with many organizations, CCT's manufacturing sites continue to operate in person, but most of its general administrative and sales force employees are working remotely and following strict safety protocols due to Covid-19. The majority of CCT employees who continue to work in person to create and move product are heroes in manufacturing across the medical and healthcare industry.

For the employees working remotely, the ability to keep work moving and decisions flowing is a major plus and is largely due to alignment on the company's goals, a culture of initiative, and a desire to serve customers. The downside of working remotely, besides the tedious nature of repetitive Zoom meetings, is that overwork is a real worry. It's easier to work longer, especially during off-standard hours.

CCT continues to hire globally, conducting searches, making hiring decisions, and onboarding great talent to support its growth plans. The onboarding process has shifted to nearly completely virtual and CCT has created a library of digital content that replicates the previous meet-and greet-format. Partnering with Globalization Partners has certainly reduced a lot of pressure, from HR compliance to onboarding to payroll, and has played a part in making CCT's success with its global team possible.

AFTER THE VPS, HIRE DIRECTORS TO RUN OTHER ESSENTIAL FUNCTIONS

Once you have your executive team in place within your headquarters or main global offices (assuming that team is focused on sales), the next step is to look for director-level talent. These are leaders just below VP level who are in charge of satellite offices or hubs in other parts of the country and the world.

Your VPs might be able to bring them on board, but you might have them under a different function. For example, Globalization Partners hires sales VPs in locations like London and Singapore, but our back-office functions, like technology, customer service, finance, and marketing, are often in slightly lower-cost, talent-rich jurisdictions like Ireland (one of our back-office hubs for Europe), Mexico City (our back office for the Americas) and Kuala Lumpur (our back-office hub for Asia). These are just examples, and at this point, we have many hubs. Where you can find talent is something we'll dive into in later chapters.

When you think of where to locate your back-office team, picture a bullseye around your target market (where your VP will be located) and evaluate your potential back-office locations on the basis of talent availability, time zone, and cost structure. One caveat that we've learned by witnessing our customers' experiences is that it's not ideal to hire a head of any department if the person lives in a particularly remote location, such as on a beach, no matter how appealing that talent might seem.

One of our customers learned this lesson the hard way. They had identified a superstar salesperson and hired him as their vice president of sales for all of Europe. The fact that he lived and would be working out of a remote rustic village in southern France known for its fabulous beaches did not deter them.

However, being based in a remote village made it nearly impossible for him to build relationships with key partners, who normally reside in big cities and are used to being wined and dined by people in their networks. Being hundreds of miles away from any large cities made him less successful at the time. It's questionable whether the same social dynamic will hold true post-pandemic, but the people he was supposed to be closing deals with were based in London, Munich, and other hard-charging cities—they are not hanging out on the beaches of Saint-Tropez. He was too far from his target market to have the impact they needed.

Another mistake our customers sometimes make is hiring just one salesperson in a country, without a marketing budget or team to back them up. It's nearly impossible to be successful under those conditions, no matter how skilled the new VP is. Modern marketing is digital and requires localization; hiring a sales VP without giving him or her the infrastructure to generate leads is an exercise in futility. If you're not committed to building a local demand gen team overseas, trying to set up sales offices globally is not worth it.

A better approach for our customer would have been to base their VP in London, where there are something like 10,000 high-growth tech companies, or even Amsterdam, where there are nearly 4,500. But not remote southern France, where there are far fewer high-tech prospects. If in-person meetings are required, unless someone has a strong enough existing network to build partnerships remotely, being located on Saint-Tropez (or in Tahiti) is not an asset. The choice to live in a remote "lifestyle" location also sometimes indicates that an individual is more interested in a relaxed lifestyle than success, although that reasoning may no longer be valid as remote work becomes ever more the norm.

Directors and managers oversee teams of workers producing your end product—the individual contributors in the back office responsible for making things happen. These back offices are frequently in the same time zone as your executives, but not necessarily in the same city. Back offices are typically in lower-cost jurisdictions that are adjacent to the executive talent; the executive talent needs to be closer to the movers and shakers of your industry.

The best approach when deciding where hubs should be based is to think about where your clients are located or where you know you'll have success finding the type of talent you need. Because once you have a VP in place, you'll want to hire a team to support him or her, within the same time zone, and ideally with a strong sense of collaboration. You need to add team members who can collaborate and do the work you need them to, together.

> *To be able to successfully grow into new geographic territories, if you plan on hiring an entire team in any location, you need talented leaders in place first.*

Keep in mind time zones. Setting up a hub in the same or similar time zone as your headquarters, initially, is useful for productivity. This same strategy is necessary as you go global with your sales and customer support teams.

For us, one of our first non-U.S. hubs was Mexico City. After hiring directors in various functions to manage the local office, we proceeded to hire over 100 people there in multiple roles. We also have an HR team locally reporting to our HQ HR team. The reason we opted for Mexico is the abundant talent, lower cost structure, and similar time zone to Boston and San Diego, where our U.S. sales and customer support teams are based. When we first opened our Mexico City office, hiring employees there cost much less than hiring in the U.S. or Canada, however, that has quickly changed since the 2020 pandemic. Since then, we have expanded our team to include telephone salespeople, content writers, finance team members, lawyers, analysts, and engineers. The quality of work and passionate contributions delivered by our team members who reside in Mexico is the highest caliber. We also continue to hire widely in the U.S., especially in strategic roles for which American talent is highly valued, such as interfacing with the U.S. market and various executive roles.

CHOOSING YOUR FIRST HUB

Once you know that you want to expand globally, your first step after filling your executive market-facing seats should be to evaluate the locations you might want to consider for your corresponding back-office hub.

Time Zone

First, consider where you want your brain trust for the region to be based. Then look at time zones to ascertain locations the office could be located and still be convenient to collaborate with.

If you're planning to enter Europe, for example, you'd likely want to look at London, Amsterdam, or maybe Berlin as your European market-facing locations where you'd hire a VP, because they are major cities where your market-facing executives will need to take meetings.

From there, consider the back office. For Europe, you might consider Dublin, Romania, Poland, Barcelona, or other locations that are hubs of talent. Key factors in choice of location for a back-office hub include availability of talent, time zone, and language capabilities of the local talent pool, along with the cost structure and administrative hurdles related to local hires.

Language

Regarding language requirements, do you need English-speaking employees, or does your client base require people who speak French, Spanish, or German, for example?

Globalization Partners chose Ireland as its first European back-office base because it's five hours ahead of Eastern Standard Time, a short flight from major cities in Europe—but is a lower-cost city compared to London—and the talent pool is high performing and English speaking. Many residents in Ireland speak multiple languages, so it's a great gateway to Europe in terms of serving clients in other countries.

Subsequently, we built hubs in Belfast and Poland because we needed access to more talent, and in the case of Poland, we needed a base farther east. Poland also has a lot of technologists, and most professionals are multilingual.

At some point, given the nature of our business model and the fact that we have entities everywhere, we flung open the doors and started hiring everyone, everywhere. That is the true access to talent, and one that can only be afforded with use of an extremely competent Employer of Record. We have seen many companies begin to take this approach in the era of global remote work and with the use of our platform.

Cost

Cost was the original reason that we chose to base large numbers of our back-office team members in Mexico City, compared to hiring everyone in Boston and San Francisco. Cost is typically one of the first factors companies consider when deciding where to place a hub office. For us, we knew the talent was there and the cost was so much less than hiring everyone in tech hubs that it made sense to set up shop in Mexico City. Besides that obvious benefit, we have come to love Mexico City, and our many colleagues there. There's a vibrancy and a warmth to Mexican culture, and our colleagues have brought much joy to our business, along with their radical competence.

Lower cost was also a reason we set up shop in India, where we now have more than 100 highly skilled employees supporting our business, mostly behind the scenes in our finance and marketing departments. The only downsides of having employees in India are 1) the time zone difference and 2) the poor infrastructure, which makes Wi-Fi and internet service a bit less stable. However, our team in India (like the teams of many of our customers) is extraordinary, and the value they bring to our company is as exceptional as they are. Like Mexico, our team in India is composed of very special people; the opportunity to share a slice of Indian culture and life has brought color, community, and vibrancy to our company. Beyond that, our team members in India are highly strategic and ambitious—they bring a lot to the business.

Cost is a critical factor to consider even during periods of high growth, in case there is an unexpected downturn. One company we know was growing exponentially and hiring anyone they found who met their criteria. They had been growing extremely fast, hiring at a rate of about three employees a week to keep up with demand; cost and location had been the least of their worries.

Suddenly, when Covid-19 hit, demand shrank and they had to terminate many of those highly paid employees they had just brought on board because they were seen as overpaid for what they were delivering compared to employees in lower-cost jurisdictions. Not only did that process of terminating employees grind any growth to a complete halt, but, more importantly, it damaged morale among the employees who remained. It took a number of months to rebound.

Now they're rebuilding with our help and making more strategic decisions about where employees should be based, with an eye toward hiring talent in lower-cost areas where it makes sense to do so. Their goal is to build the company with an appropriate cost structure in mind at the outset so that they're never forced to restructure their company again. Besides the cost of terminating a significant portion of a company's workforce, the emotional toll of terminating people to cut costs is extreme. We believe it's better to structure a team for efficiency at the outset and, also, to reward your team for work well done and to pay above market compensation when you have discovered great talent in any location.

Hiring in lower-cost areas is a big trend right now, both in the U.S. and globally. Instead of hiring in San Francisco, we're seeing sales teams being located in Park City, Utah, or Austin, just as companies are evaluating places like the Philippines and Estonia for their global hiring plans.

Of note, choosing locations *only* because they are low-cost is not a winning formula. Think carefully, because hiring people in a place where they can't be successful and you can't work reliably with them is a losing strategy for all involved. Beyond that, compensation in lower-cost hubs will rise quickly. Within several years, I believe there will be an equalization of compensation globally, as companies continue to compete for talent.

Talent Pool

We've found that one key to effectively choosing your first non-U.S. site is to be sure the city has a large enough talent pool to draw from when building your team there. Even if remote work becomes the norm worldwide post-pandemic, it's still ideal to have centralized workspaces where employees can meet, even occasionally. Typically, if you can hire one director-level person, he or she can fill that team *from that same city* with his or her network. We take the approach that 10 people in one location can be easier to manage than 10 people in 10 locations, although many of our customers are indeed successfully taking advantage of the opportunity to literally hire anyone, anywhere.

Once you have a team in place in another city, you have the opportunity to grow a referral network from your own employees. Offer a referral bonus to people you've already hired for attracting like-minded, hard-working job candidates. That way, your employees become your initial qualifiers, determining who in their circle of contacts would be a good fit for the work your company needs done.

Adding to an initial team in a new city is also efficient in terms of the learning curve to manage the cultural nuance of that location. Once you've mastered familiarity with your local team's work style, it might be most efficient to continue applying that knowledge rather than moving to an entirely new country and having to learn all the local laws, customs, and even holidays there. Leverage that new expertise you've just developed in one city as much as you can, but don't hesitate to start building your team even further in a new location when you're ready. Why not, with the world as your oyster?

Culture-Building

One reason we love having "hubs" from which to hire people is that having multiple employees based in one location also allows them to foster culture and collaboration—rather than building a team of disconnected professionals who have to try to work together from afar. The team that plays together, stays together, and even in the era of global remote work, it remains true. Our team in Ireland recently took an ocean plunge together in February. That would have been hard to do if literally everyone was remote, and while everyone couldn't be there, we loved the pictures.

Another factor to keep in mind is country culture. Your company has its own internal culture, and as you set up locations in other countries, the local culture will impact your organization's culture. It's a natural progression. One key thing I've learned is to set the tone right from the top. In the early days of hiring new country managers, I would personally have a call with the soon-to-be-hired country director and explain exactly what I expected: fairness and kindness paired with sky-high standards; integrity; my philosophy of the triple bottom line; and diversity in our offices, with equal opportunity for all. The direct messaging worked, and many of those managers still refer back to those early phone calls to this day. We also have an extremely diverse company, in countries where that is far from the norm, and a company spirit that honors the uniqueness of each amazing person who has built it.

Infrastructure

How solid a country's infrastructure is, meaning electricity and internet access, should be considered when evaluating potential hub locations.

Most major cities around the world have reliable internet, but not all. Island nations, for example, may be strong on many counts but lack reliable internet. That one fact may make that locale less desirable if you need to have regular contact with employees there (and you will). Some locations are able to navigate around this by virtue of everyone going to the office. In situations like this, you might need to be aware that not everyone can reliably work from home. Defer to your local country manager to advise on this. If you don't have one, our sales and HR teams are always on standby for prospective customers with questions like that.

THYCOTIC

Thycotic is the leading provider of cloud-ready privilege-management solutions that protect an organization's most valuable assets from both cyberattacks and insider threats. Thycotic's security tools empower over 12,500 organizations, from small businesses to the Fortune 100, to limit privileged account risk, implement least privilege policies, control applications, and demonstrate compliance.

Headquartered in Washington, D.C., Thycotic operates worldwide with offices in the UK and Australia and more than 500 employees.

In 2020, Thycotic recorded an 87 percent year-over-year increase in cloud sales growth, along with the addition of more than 500 new cloud customers, bringing the total to more than 1,200. Thycotic also witnessed 28 percent growth in channel sales from global markets in 2020 as a result of its ongoing commitment to innovation.

The company's first international employee was the senior vice president of sales, who was hired in the UK in 2016. Thycotic's focus was initially on the UK, Western Europe, and Australian markets and then rapidly expanded into Eastern Europe, the Middle East, and APAC. The business currently employs 180 staff members in 23 countries, most of whom work remotely.

After pivoting to remote work for nearly all staff members during the Covid-19 pandemic, Thycotic found that employees are just as productive working from home, but most look forward to returning to the collaboration that in-person meetings facilitate. The upside of remote work is feeling more of a work-life balance. They spend what used to be commuting time doing other things like cooking, exercising, or pursuing a hobby.

Employees are proud to have helped other businesses during the pandemic, as with so many remote workers, existing security risks are magnified and many new attack vectors are introduced. This forced IT and security operations groups to quickly provide secure solutions and strategies for remote workers to access internal applications, which is exactly what Thycotic does.

Thycotic was able to grow as much as it has internationally during the past four years with a fully remote workforce, and to exceed its annual growth plans, by having the right technology tools to connect people, the right security practices for the business to protect its data, and a culture of trust, connection, and common purpose. It also has excellent local HR support everywhere it has local team members, via Globalization Partners, to supplement its in-house team. For example, many team members are remote throughout the U.S. and the UK, but employees report they are so connected throughout each day by quick video calls or through Slack that it's almost as if they are sitting in the same office. That's when you know it's working.

PRESSURE FROM CUSTOMERS

Of course, if you have a major customer who is demanding that you hire someone local to serve them, that one driver is likely to trump all the other factors—cost, talent pool, time zone, and everything else. If a customer who accounts for a significant portion of your corporate revenue, or has the potential to contribute a significant portion, requests that you hire someone close to them as their liaison with your company, you should seriously consider the request. That employee could be in a sales role, a customer service role, a tech support role, or something else, depending on what product or service you provide your customer.

Customers in some countries may feel strongly about having a local representative, whereas other countries may not care if you serve them from a U.S. office. For example, companies in France place a high value on having access to a local French employee, whereas in Canada, you're less likely to hear a specific request for an employee based there if you're already based elsewhere in North America.

DECIDE (BROADLY) ON LOCATION FIRST, THEN CHOOSE PEOPLE

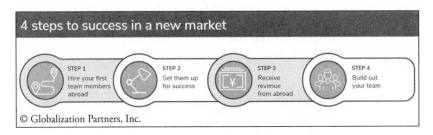

4 steps to success in a new market

STEP 1 Hire your first team members abroad

STEP 2 Set them up for success

STEP 3 Receive revenue from abroad

STEP 4 Build out your team

© Globalization Partners, Inc.

Companies that have the fastest success in expanding globally start by thinking about their geographic plan or goals. They strategize where their target customers are and, therefore, where they should base a team of employees to support those customers. They evaluate who needs to work with those customers in person and who can be in a hub office in the same time zone working remotely. Successful companies go where the business is, or where the talent pool exists.

As we look to the future, organizations that limit their hiring to only people who want to go to a company's offices five days a week are going to be dinosaurs. Growing a network of contacts that spans the globe and collaborates digitally is the wave of the future and will be required for success.

ADDITIONAL RESOURCES

You'll find more information about recommended geographic hiring sequences at globaltalentunleashed.com/chapter-3

CHAPTER 4

Setting Up Legal Entities

Companies that don't choose to use a global employment platform go the more traditional route of registering their company for business in every jurisdiction where they do business. About 90 percent of the time, the first trigger for "doing business" in a new jurisdiction is the hire of the first employee in that location. The step-by-step process of setting up a business location in another country can vary greatly. In some countries, the process is simple and straightforward, and in others, lengthy and convoluted.

Take Brazil, for example. Brazil is a growing market in Latin America, and many companies consider setting up an office there. Many local advisors will recommend either retaining an Employer of Record or incorporating a branch office or a subsidiary in-country prior to hiring that first employee.

To incorporate, you need to find several service providers: 1) a good local attorney who is willing to act as your legal representative there and assume legal liability for any missteps you may make; 2) an accountant and; 3) a tax advisor. With those advisors on board, you need to set up a physical office in the country, via a coworking provider at the very least, including leasing a registered address with local furnished office space.

As part of the incorporation process, you also need a locally compliant bank account. Being locally compliant means that significant shareholders in the company must present themselves and their passports at the bank to prove their identities. This step makes it harder for venture-backed or equity-backed companies because the banks often want to meet everyone in person who owns more than 10 percent of the company. There may be other documents to file, too, because banks are financially and legally responsible for making sure that they follow careful anti-money laundering procedures. Banks are generally reluctant to set up bank accounts for international companies because of this, and, frankly, they know that the amount of money passing through a subsidiary intended solely to hire a few people is negligible from a business perspective. If the bank is caught inadvertently funneling funds related to terrorism or other illegal activities, it can be shut down. With repercussions so severe, it's understandable that banks are reluctant to put their organization on the line, unless it can guarantee that your business is aboveboard and that there will be sufficient money flowing through it to be worth their while. Otherwise, they typically won't be motivated to assist (and understandably so). For this reason, setting up the local bank account is usually the most frustrating part of setting up international subsidiaries, at least for private companies.

Once your bank account is established, there are capitalization requirements, or funds that must be deposited in the local account for the new subsidiary to be considered incorporated. After the corporation is established, you then need to register it for corporate taxes and value-added taxes, and register as an employer so that you can run payroll. Once payroll is set up, you need to figure out which Collective Bargaining Agreements apply to your industry or employees; set up health and dental benefits for your employees, and manage approximately a million other minor details.

The standard process of incorporating in Brazil generally takes almost a year to complete and thousands of emails; other countries can take anywhere from three to 12 months total. That's all before you can even begin to start recruiting for open positions in that office.

The amount of administrative complexity to hire people internationally in the traditional method is a huge barrier to hiring overseas, which is what makes the Employer of Record model so compelling. Of course, it can be worth setting up in-house for a larger local operation, but most companies now prefer to use an Employer of Record when hiring less than 25 people in any given location.

CONCERNS ABOUT COMPLIANCE

As you begin to plan for adding employees in other countries to your payroll, you'll also want to choose an Employer of Record that guarantees hiring in accordance with local employment law and best practice, or ensure that you set up your own contracts with global and local expertise. Hiring team members via locally compliant employment contracts is essential for protecting the business from liability. Contracts that are not in compliance with local regulations essentially provide no protection to the employer at all; terms in an employment contract that violate local employee protections are deemed void and unenforceable by local courts. Agreements that are consistent with U.S. law are immaterial in Brazil, or any other country for that matter. Only local laws matter in that jurisdiction.

Further, in many countries, the only valid employment contracts are the versions in the legal language of that country; English-language translations are also considered invalid.

Many years ago, I had a customer who wanted to hire a high-flying salesperson in France. He decided to go the low-cost route and registered his U.S. company as an employer in-country (definitely not recommended, because it means the U.S. company is liable for everything the employee does in France and may also trigger a corporate taxable presence of U.S. company revenues in France). I recommended that, if he chose that route, he at least work with a local employment attorney to put a locally compliant employment contract in place. The cost was US$5,000, and he almost choked at the idea. I warned him that it would be money well-spent, but he ignored my advice and hired the employee with the same offer letter he used for his U.S. employees.

Unfortunately, within days, it was apparent that the new VP of sales was not going to be the rainmaker they'd hoped. Indeed, the employee was bombastic to work with and hardly showed up to a day of work before he was making trouble. They reviewed the employment contract, which was completely irrelevant in France, and the employee knew it. Since there was no locally compliant employment contract, there was no legally agreed probation period. It took a few months for the company to make the decision to terminate the employee, but they ended up paying him almost two years' worth of salary by the time they finished—not to mention a tremendous amount of legal work and administrative headaches. If they had used our global employment platform (and thus we would have hired him via our locally compliant employment contract), they could have terminated the employee during the probation period and essentially walked away.

Some of the most important elements of that employment contract you'll want addressed are the IP, non-compete, and confidentiality clauses. These are the clauses that state that any IP developed by the employee is transferred to the employer; under what terms the employee can work with a competitor; and what information must be protected by the employee as a trade secret. Some of the worst situations companies find themselves in are realizing that they simply assumed their U.S.-based IP agreement clauses, non-compete, and confidentially clauses were fine in whatever countries they hired employees—or forgot to get it in writing in the first place. Ascertaining that you don't actually own the IP that your employees built a few days before your IPO is a surefire deal-killer. Unfortunately, this word of warning goes back to the concept of "buyer beware." Underinvesting in legal infrastructure, or underinvesting in whatever Employer of Record solution you choose, is a real problem when it comes down to things like who owns your IP and whether your employees have to maintain your trade secrets. We've seen situations where companies don't have properly translated protection clauses in place, and literally lose much of the value they thought they had built in their business. American businesses have fairly stringent notions about protecting idea ownership that aren't necessarily the cultural norm in many places; it's critical to have actual agreements in place that are compliant and enforceable in the countries where the employees live.

Should a company choose the old-fashioned route of setting up a subsidiary or a branch office overseas, the work is not finished upon incorporating or setting up payroll. The entity has to be managed just like any other company around the globe, in accordance with local regulations. There are monthly financial statements to be run in the local language and tax returns that have to be filed with local, state, and national tax authorities. Companies must also determine how to break out profit that is specifically attributed to that one location for tax purposes. For example, if you have a customer service rep providing phone support from Brazil to customers in other countries, that rep may not be generating revenue directly, but you'll need to ascribe some income to Brazil to justify having the office there. In many cases, you end up taking your best guess, with the help of your local tax advisors, but figuring out the web of global tax issues often requires a very senior, full-time dedicated resource—or a team of resources, depending on your business.

TESTING THE WATERS

That's not to say that you necessarily have to expand into a new country with plans to build a hub there. Sometimes setting up shop in a new location is useful for market research. A major payments firm, for example, wanted to expand into Africa a few years ago, but management wasn't sure which country made the most sense. So, an executive committed US$1 million to exploring 10 different locations. The company hired 10 people in 10 different cities via our global employment platform in order to see which would be the most successful in building a market and a business and gave each a nominal budget. Within a year, not only did they know which markets would be successful, but they were significantly further along than they would have been if they had only been doing market research— they had 10 employees on the ground who showed remarkable success with measurable results. This was made easy and possible by virtue of our global employment platform, since the company didn't have to incorporate in each country prior to testing the waters.

But multinational payment companies aren't the only companies to test out international locations by placing employees in-country. OneStream Software, which was already operating in several global markets, decided it wanted to test South Africa as a new market by placing an employee there. Likewise, ClickDimensions took a similar approach in deciding to test the market in Australia, hiring on the opposite side of the world from its Atlanta headquarters.

Testing the waters by hiring one employee is a legitimate market research approach. The time and effort required to bring that one employee on board via an Employer of Record is nominal and unbelievably value-adding to your entire company and team.

Dataiku

Dataiku, an advanced enterprise AI platform, was established in Paris by French founders. The company then expanded into two high-growth markets—the UK, followed by the U.S. Today, the company is headquartered in New York City and employs almost 600 staff members.

Although the company's initial global expansion involved moving into the UK and U.S., the latter of which has become one of its largest market opportunities, its more recent expansion into the Asia-Pacific region is contributing significantly to its continued growth. Going global enabled Dataiku to grow more quickly and sell in new regions.

The pivoting required in response to Covid-19 resulted in Dataiku having all of its employees work remotely, though offices are open.

That remote option is expected to remain in effect until the fall of 2021. Becoming a remote workforce has been difficult, with many employees working longer hours, since there is no clear distinction between work and personal life, and people are taking fewer vacations, prompting concerns about burnout. The ramp-up time is also longer for new hires, especially those early in their careers.

One of the most positive outcomes of the pandemic has been that Dataiku has become bolder in trying new markets now that everyone is working remotely anyway. Hiring in India is now underway with plans to soon enter the Japanese market. The company says it's not sure it would have tried to tackle those markets before Covid-19 made global remote work its internal norm.

DECIDING WHICH ROLES TO SOURCE WHERE

As you're starting to think through your global hiring plan, it's important to recognize that not all roles within your organization make sense for "everyone, everywhere," or to locate far from headquarters or the target customer base. For example, your U.S. sales team should probably remain in the U.S., culturally and linguistically, from a time zone perspective close to its target clientele. It probably makes sense for your C-Suite to be aligned around a fairly short window of time zones so that you can easily collaborate during normal business hours to the extent possible. But so many other roles can be located anywhere. Your back-office functions, from accounting to finance to logistics, marketing content, IT, and others could potentially be located in much less expensive jurisdictions, where there's a great opportunity to hire excellent talent at much lower costs than you can hire around your HQ office.

What to Consider Before Expanding

Culture

- Does the product or service add value to the local markets?
- Do you understand those who live in the community?

Legal and regulatory barriers

- Can your business work within the local laws and regulations?
- Do you have a legal team that can review and identify possible barriers?

Government procedures

- What are the currency exchanges rates?
- Can you gain access to the necessary resources and materials?
- Do they have protection policies for businesses?

Business case

- Can you provide justification for undertaking this expansion?
- Is your business capable of responding to the challenges of expanding overseas?

Consider performing:
- Market studies
- Financial feasibility studies

Sometimes it also makes sense to hire people in multiple locations so that the team in Asia can be working while your North America team sleeps. I've often sent projects I was working on late at night to my Asia team and woke up to them being completed—just a bit of magic of having a team on which the sun never sets.

When we talk about hiring talent outside your home location, we're not talking about hiring freelancers or independent contractors. If you determine that you need support from full-time workers in another state or country, they should be classified as employees. Most employment laws recognize anyone who is working full-time for an organization or under the direction and control of that organization (whether part-time or full-time) as an employee, who is then protected by local labor laws. Trying to skirt local laws by retaining freelancers can result in harsh and expensive punishment if that worker is dedicated solely to supporting your company or your company is directing the work of that individual.

Beyond that, freelancers are always looking for other work. For companies that need fully dedicated, highly trained professionals, it's still generally much more scalable to hire full team members and treat them according to the respect they deserve, and the protections provided to them under the law.

Some countries barely recognize the concept of independent contractors, with the default classification being employee. In many countries, residents are well-informed regarding their rights and will ultimately use these rights as leverage with an employer who has misclassified them. Employee whistleblowing (which happens a lot and ultimately drives a lot of businesses to our doors so that we can help with the cleanup) results in social charges, fines, and penalties that can amount to as much as 50 percent of the annual cost of employment, plus major tax and legal repercussions in the countries where companies have been paying people under the table. The risks of misclassifying employees or paying people illegally via gross payments and bank wires is huge, with major liability if you get caught. It is almost always wiser to engage individuals who are properly classified as employees. It's easy enough with the Employer of Record industry in place to do it right, and I highly recommend that you do it right in the first place. Of course, if you're reading this and worried about "skeletons in the closet," fear not—we have an entire team dedicated to helping our customers clean skeletons out of the closet before their big exits or IPOs. It's an expensive and time-consuming process and your employees will know they have leverage, so my recommendation is to invest in a competent Employer of Record at the outset, or build your own in-house subsidiaries if you prefer to go it alone.

WHERE TO LOCATE YOUR BACK-OFFICE HUBS

When determining where to set up your back-office hubs, the first consideration is customer needs. What level of support do they need, and where is the most appropriate location given the talent availability for the roles you need and the time zones in which you require collaboration?

Because collaboration between customers and offices is generally important, you'll want to factor in:

- Availability of talent

- Time zones to ensure there is overlap when people are in the office and available to work collaboratively, or with customers

- English-language capabilities among talent in that jurisdiction to facilitate communication with HQ and internationally (assuming your lengua franca is English)

- Culture: does the local work style match your expectations, and is it easy to accommodate differences in communication styles?

- Talent pool familiar with a standard of work inside high-growth companies—that is, has experience at similarly sized brands or companies

- Cost of compensation in that jurisdiction: I don't recommend going for the lowest-cost jurisdiction to sacrifice talent availability or quality, but it does factor in and can be a major driver

- Economic and geopolitical stability, including currency volatility, which can create complications

- Business-friendly government: how easy is it to get things done when you need them; how challenging is the local labor legislation?

- Infrastructure: Wi-Fi reliability, internet access, distance to an international airport

Volatile currency exchange rates become an issue when you're paying employees in the local currency and the value of the compensation they're paid regularly fluctuates. This is why in Argentina, for example, employees push hard to be paid in U.S. dollars, which is a more stable currency. We don't blame them—some years ago, our local employees told us that bakeries in Buenos Aires were writing prices on chalkboards so they could change the price of bread every hour. The local economy is now stabilizing, but employees still prefer to be paid in U.S. dollars.

Globalization Partners accommodates this in various ways when appropriate, such as a peg to a currency, where we can, but it can come with challenges. If you agree to pay an employee's compensation in a non-local currency, the employee's local taxes and social security still must be paid in local currency. And that number, against the dollar, fluctuates regularly, leaving the net amount that lands in the employee's bank account to change each month. Which exchange rate should apply when it comes to things like expense reports and payroll? For example, if an employee incurs expenses throughout the month, the exchange rate on the day of a given expense will be different from the rate on the day the company sends reimbursement as well as the day the funds land in the employee's account. The employer cannot track every day's exchange rate. Even small amounts can become a constant source of irritation to the employee, who might not understand how the global bank rates work.

In places with highly fluctuating currencies, Globalization Partners' solution has been to review, and then proactively address, the fluctuations every six months rather than constantly negotiating net pay with employees. We also recommend always being a little generous; err on the side of the employees because it matters much more to them and is worth the well-being of your employer/employee relationship. Most employees are satisfied with this, but it is always a point of worry at the early stage of negotiating with candidates. Employees, understandably, want to make sure that their compensation is secure against the uncertainties they have to deal with. Likewise, good employers want to be accommodating but also need to make sure that they're following the law.

Of note, negotiating a fixed exchange rate from the employee's compensation currency to U.S. dollars only makes sense in locations where employees really do live in a highly volatile economy with rampant inflation—which is not a common situation. The euro, pound, and dollar all fluctuate against each other, but in most locations, dealing with currency fluctuations doesn't have any real impact on an employee's life. Some employers are occasionally asked to fix an exchange rate for negotiated compensation to dollars in places where it doesn't make sense, like Europe or Hong Kong. We suggest avoiding doing this when it is not necessary and holding your ground. Argentina is the only modern economy where we see this regularly.

As you set up your international hub, keep your exit strategy in mind. That is, do you plan to eventually go public, sell, or be acquired? If any of those are among the possible goals you're working toward, it's essential that you do business legally and according to world-class compliance standards everywhere you have a presence. Taking shortcuts by hiring contractors when they should be classified as employees, not acknowledging or paying corporate taxes, or failing to transfer to the company the intellectual property your employees create is likely to derail future efforts to exit.

No one wants to acquire a business that has been operating illegally or doesn't actually own what it thinks it does. This is one of the core value-adds our customers find in our platform—essentially, they're leveraging us to make sure that they can focus on growth without worrying about the legal, tax, and HR nuances of hiring people in 187 countries.

Set up your company legitimately from the start so as not to jeopardize the future success of the business, however you define that.

Establishing a hub location is a strategy for expansion that enables you to put down roots with a single employee and then grow your presence in that area with additional hiring. When you reach a point where your hiring needs exceed the availability of specialized talent in that market, it's time to look to your next hub location. Hubs become local networks of your team members that serve your customers in that region, as well as the U.S. operation and other specialized hubs.

ADDITIONAL RESOURCES

You'll find more information to help determine what is best for your company at globaltalentunleashed.com/chapter-4

CHAPTER 5

Using an Employer of Record

An Employer of Record is a company that is already doing business in the country in which you want to operate and can serve as the legal employer of the local talent you want to hire. Employers of Record can hire, onboard, and then manage the employee relationship, taking responsibility for payroll, taxes, and benefits. Because they're legally the employers, they're responsible for ensuring that everything is compliant. This should, if the contracts are all structured correctly, ensure that the employee is being engaged via fully compliant local employment options. A truly world-class global Employer of Record will take it a step further and ensure not only that local law is being followed but also that best practices maximize the protection of the end customer in terms of non-compete, data security, cybersecurity, IP agreements, and other details. Because the global Employer of Record industry is quite new, it's important for customers to carefully vet the Employer of Record that they choose.

While the Employer of Record is responsible for all of the employee management activities, the customer is the employee's direct supervisor and is in charge of work assignments. The relationship can be similar to that of a temporary employment agency, however, the Employer of Record industry is designed for full-time, permanent employees, usually in highly professional roles. The Employer of Record manages all human resources and payroll tasks and leaves the employer to focus on overseeing the employee's day-to-day work.

> *Given the large startup costs, in time and money, if your hope is to start with a small team that builds, and time is of the essence, then a competent Employer of Record can help you bypass all of the typical required paperwork and get up and running quickly with far less of an initial investment.*

The biggest advantage to employers is that the Employer of Record often eliminates the need to set up a company and run payroll in-house when hiring your first team member in a country. The Employer of Record should assume all the risks associated with ensuring that their structure for hiring the employees in another country is compliant and handled well. In addition, through an Employer of Record, you can hire global employees in hours rather than spending months trying to figure out how to do so. Be careful to review the master service agreement with the Employer of Record, however, because terms and conditions can vary. Some small Employer of Record firms state in the contract that all liability passes through to the end customer, and they cut other corners as well. Buyer beware!

ACTIVPAYROLL

Activpayroll is a leading global professional service organization, providing integrated global and domestic payroll solutions, expatriate taxation services, global HR services, and online HR management tools to over 1,200 companies in more than 150 countries. With offices in Edinburgh, Singapore, Florida, Frankfurt, Isle of Man, Paris, Orléans, Dubai, Dublin, Cape Town, Perth, Australia, and global HQ in Aberdeen, Scotland, activpayroll has one of the largest and most experienced international payroll and expatriate tax teams in the world. The company's customers range from local charities to some of the world's biggest household names.

Throughout the course of the pandemic, its focus has been solely on protecting its workforce of more than 240 employees while adhering to government legislation in each international jurisdiction in which it operates. Nearly 100 percent of its global workforce continues to work remotely from home for the near future.

Remote working has resulted in both positive and negative experiences for the business and for its most important asset—its people. Although working remotely has the obvious benefits of no commuting time or costs and, in many cases, a better work-life balance, there are downsides, too, such as lack of space within the home for remote working, potential feelings of isolation for employees who live alone, the difficulty of juggling home and family life, the challenges of creating a structured work-life balance (with the laptop always at hand), and the general lack of interaction with colleagues and peers.

The other very positive message from a business and commercial perspective is that the level and method of interaction between employees and customers has increased. Through the use of video and camera-enabled virtual meeting platforms, the ability to "see" customers and to "meet" their service teams and put a face to a name has strengthened many business relationships.

In any service industry, continuing to provide an excellent experience to customers is paramount, and intrinsically linked to that is ensuring that employees remain engaged, motivated, healthy, happy, and safe.

Although most international expansions start as part of an organization's strategic vision, Covid-19 has resulted in many businesses expanding into new territories, sometimes without them actually knowing it. Allowing employees to be close to their families and loved ones during the pandemic has caused some employers to have a fragmented and widely spread employee population, with many employees now conducting business in jurisdictions where the employer has no legal entity, physicality, or other presence.

Typically, employees have continued to be paid from their regular payroll and have continued to be subject to local statutory employment tax withholdings (income tax and social security primarily) throughout the period of working remotely from home. This decision was taken simply on the basis that, again, this absence from "the office" was a short-term, temporary arrangement and, therefore, continuing with the status quo as far as payroll and withholdings is concerned was the correct course of action. However, as of the end of 2020, companies realized that they needed to get in line from a compliance standpoint. Any employee who works remotely in a jurisdiction (a different international location) other than their normal place of work and has done so since the beginning of the pandemic has almost certainly created some kind of employment tax and payroll-related implication for both themselves and their legal employer.

This has caused many of activpayroll's customers of all shapes and sizes, across all industry sectors, all around the world, to unexpectedly face a significant problem from an employment tax and payroll perspective. Employers now have a remote workforce who have spent almost a year, in some cases, working from home, and undertaking their duties of employment—in many cases in locations where the only presence or physicality the employer has in that location is the employees themselves.

Therefore, while working remotely from home is very likely to continue in some form even after life returns to "normal," employers must be mindful of the flexible working arrangements they put in place for the long term, particularly when these arrangements permit employees to work from an international location other than the "normal" and previous work location.

In simple terms, location of payroll and contractual arrangements with an employing entity do not determine the income tax and social security liabilities for remote workers, and many of activpayroll's diverse client base are embarking on the journey of introducing specific remote working policies and frameworks to ensure first and foremost that both the company and the remote workers are fully compliant from an employment tax and payroll perspective but also endeavoring to offer as much flexibility as possible to encourage the working from home and work-life balance philosophy.

In many cases, activpayroll establishes a new payroll for that customer in the new location. When not feasible or preferable to the customer, the customer is recommended to Globalization Partners, which enables companies to hire anyone, anywhere, without setting up their own internal payroll registrations.

Another potential advantage of an Employer of Record is having access to an astute legal team familiar with local employment law. This has proven extremely valuable for a number of Globalization Partners customers. One UK-based company discovered that value quickly when one of its employees got drunk during a work trip and then posted on social media. The company started moving to immediately terminate him, which could have been costly, but instead consulted Globalization Partners first. This was appropriate, since Globalization Partners was the Employer of Record and the situation was our responsibility to handle. Despite the UK's strict labor laws, Globalization Partners was able to immediately terminate the employee and managed a quick resolution to the situation without causing major issues for the customer—and without the company having to navigate the complexities of UK labor law from afar.

In another situation, a new employee took some vacation time to visit Canada, failing to mention that he was immigrating. Upon arrival, he resigned from his position and asked that his unused vacation time be paid out to him with his last paycheck. The customer consulted with its Globalization Partners team (which is part of our service), and we recognized that because the former employee was in breach of his contract, he was not entitled to vacation pay. In fact, the company was able to charge him back for failing to give proper notice and for the work he failed to complete, saving the company considerable resources.

But there are many other advantages of using an Employer of Record beyond legal oversight and guidance.

The table below provides a quick comparison of setting up a branch or subsidiary in order to do business in another country versus working with an already-established Employer of Record.

	SET UP NEW LOCATION	EMPLOYER OF RECORD (EOR)
Costs	Typically include, but are not limited to, incorporation, local capital requirements, tax and legal advisor fees, and payroll costs, among others.	Include a setup fee for each employee and a retained service fee, typically based on the employee's salary.
Banking requirements	Opening a new bank account prior to setting up a new payroll may require a minimum deposit and an in-person meeting between bankers and shareholders to prove identity.	The EOR already has a bank account established through which employees are paid.
Timeframe	The average time required to set up a new office is between two and six months. To complete this, you will need to hire legal, financial, tax, and payroll advisors to guide you.	A high-quality EOR can onboard new employees in a matter of hours.
Taxes	As part of setting up your local entity, you'll need to determine the corporate and payroll tax laws and filing requirements for the location to ensure you are in compliance.	The EOR should be responsible for paying all appropriate payroll taxes.
Compliance	To be sure that your company is always in compliance with local laws and regulations, you'll want to retain advisors to navigate data privacy laws, employment laws, tax laws, and others.	A quality EOR is contractually responsible for compliance related to the employment law.

	SET UP NEW LOCATION	EMPLOYER OF RECORD (EOR)
Contracts, employment agreements and legal terms with employees	Before hiring employees, you'll want to tailor your employment contracts and IP/non-compete/confidentiality agreements to ensure compliance with local labor laws. You should also ascertain if you're subject to union regulations and legally required to have handbooks, and handle any other local requirements from an HR perspective. Terminating workers must also be done according to local laws and can risk lawsuits if done improperly.	A high-quality EOR is responsible for providing a locally compliant employment contract, protecting the customer according to best business practices, following all HR laws including provision of local handbooks, managing union relationships, and, when needed, managing the onboarding and separation process so that country-specific onboarding and termination procedures are followed.
Cultural barriers	To understand local culture and negotiate with employees, it can be useful to hire local human resource experts.	High-quality EORs employ local experts familiar with area culture and customs, to aid in any cultural barriers.
Benefits	Benefits are an essential piece of any employment package, but the cost per employee can be exorbitant if hiring only one or two professionals.	High-quality EORs should have already developed competitive benefits packages that match the benefits of the country where the business is based. Ideally, they also access packages with economies of scale.

Before you decide which expansion approach makes the most sense, it may help to ask these five key questions:

- How quickly do I intend to start hiring in a new location, and am I committed to a very significant presence from Day 1? (For example, setting up a factory or manufacturing hub, or local retail stores.)

- Do I have other operations in that country, besides just hiring people?

- Am I ready to fully commit to a new market?

- Is time-to-hire a factor?

- Will the risk of incompliance slow down or delay my ability to move quickly in hiring the talent I want?

When your plans to hire a few people in a new country are as simple as that, you're hiring a team of remote workers, or you're just testing the waters prior to a larger expansion, most companies find that working with an Employer of Record saves time and money and reduces risk. Given the large startup costs, in time and money, if your hope is to start with a small team that builds, and time is of the essence, then an Employer of Record can help you bypass all of the typical required paperwork and get you up and running quickly with far less of an initial investment. You can always set up your own infrastructure later, if it makes sense—although many of our customers use our solution on a permanent basis.

RESIDE WORLDWIDE

Headquartered in Seattle, Washington, RESIDE Worldwide, Inc. is the leading provider of professionally operated and managed global alternative accommodations, with a portfolio of premier hospitality and technology brands, including ABODA by RESIDE, Broadway Plaza, The Beekman Tower, The Residences at W New York, The Oxford, OnBase Suites, and 3SIXTY. RESIDE's mission is to present a new way to stay, offering a curated experience to guests no matter the destination or duration of their stay.

RESIDE aggregated a world-class partner network of over one million of the best globally compliant accommodations options in more than 60 countries to satisfy growing consumer demand for high-quality, flexible, and vetted housing solutions for business or leisure travel.

Over the past three years, RESIDE has developed a comprehensive, business-ready network in the alternative accommodations industry. It is uniquely positioned to meet the rigorous demands of corporate clients and ready to capitalize on the unique economic patterns that are reflective of its business model on a global scale. Despite its demand pipeline being impacted by Covid-19, the company has still been able to grow some of its key areas of the business by pivoting to meet the changing demands of its clients. Even in a pandemic, RESIDE grew its existing global client business by 43 percent.

Due to the nature of its Fortune 100 client base, RESIDE has always had a global presence. As part of its services, the company supports clients' international relocations and finds alternative accommodations to meet their needs locally instead of expanding its footprint to match demand. In the last three years, the company added international team members in EMEA and APAC. RESIDE's considerable success in EMEA is due to its Fortune 100 clients' large European presence.

Because RESIDE is classified as an essential business, it always had a skeleton crew available to address guest needs during the pandemic. Work was also done remotely, though the breadth of remote work increased to ensure the safety of its workforce and workplace.

To keep employees connected, the business had regular weekly town hall calls with all employees. Team members have been able to have flexible work schedules where necessary to take care of children at home and still do the work. Death and illness in families are impacting people across the board.

Although the remote work model works for some, it doesn't work for all employees or roles. For that reason, it may be that RESIDE will shift to a more flexible in-office plan so that those employees who can work remotely can do so one or two days a week. All options are being considered.

While some companies ramped up their global hiring during the pandemic, RESIDE never had any discomfort with hiring team members globally because its core nature is as a global business, experiencing growth.

If your goal is to explore or test a market, or just hire a few permanent employees, investing time and energy in establishing a new business entity in that country is probably not the best use of resources. An Employer of Record allows you to forgo typical business startup tasks and get right to business, and ensure compliance—assuming you choose one that takes compliance and employee care as seriously as you do.

When competitive forces are pushing you into a new country, having to wait up to 12 months before employing people locally is a major barrier to entry. By using an Employer of Record, you can be operational in days. This enables you to hire talent quickly, make sure they're set up for success, and potentially earn first mover advantage.

Additional Resources

You'll find additional resources including guidelines on how to choose the best global employment solution at globaltalentunleashed.com/chapter-5

PART III

Regional Rollout

Depending on your global hiring plans, your first non-HQ hire may be in London, Singapore, Canada, or Mexico. Before you make that leap, however, it's a good idea to look at some of the most sought-after international regions to determine which is going to allow you to reach your goals the fastest.

Wanting to hire a sales executive to build a hub in Europe or Asia Pacific is very different from working to set up a back office to support your North America hub, and the hiring process will reflect that.

The following regional guides should help you identify the pros and cons of each target talent pool with respect to your specific goals.

CHAPTER 6

India: An Epicenter for Highly Skilled Front- and Back-Office Teams

Long known for its skilled, highly professional workforce, India remains a key region for companies in need of top talent—especially in information technology (IT) and business process outsourcing, such as accounting and finance. India is a country with many languages, including English, which is taught in schools from an early age; most of the professional class is fluent in English. Whereas the U.S., Canada, and much of Europe and other countries are facing a talent shortage, especially in engineering, India has an abundance of trained tech workers. According to the India Brand Equity Foundation, "India is the leading destination for sourcing tech talent across the world." In addition to engineers, India is also known for skilled accountants, researchers, data analysts, and other back-office staff for multinational organizations.

However, before you start making plans to set up operations in India, there are a few things you should be aware of:

CULTURE

If you're planning to build a team in India, hiring a strong local manager with experience building and managing teams for internationally headquartered companies is the best place to start. Alternately, if you're just hiring a few people, look for professionals who are used to American or European culture and workstyle—it will make communication gaps much easier to manage.

From a cultural perspective, India is incredibly warm and community centric. Where Americans are known for "living to work," it could be said that Indians are more work-life balanced and more prone to "work to live." They work hard, certainly, but family and community often take precedence over work. This is not to say that Indians are not hard-working; indeed, many of our team members in India work as hard as any of our colleagues anywhere, but there are habits in an Indian office that are unfathomable to an American team.

Our CFO was somewhat amazed when he swung through our India office and realized that our entire India office stopped and had tea together every afternoon and ate their lunches together every day as a team. This is due in part to the strong cultural foundation established by our local country director, and it's part of why our retention in India is so strong. The team feels like a family and loves being part of the community that they, and we, have built. Given that many companies have trouble with retention in India, we owe much to our local country director, Ankit Balani, for establishing a strong culture at the outset.

India is a very collective society, meaning they worry about the good of all. For that reason, finding meaning in their work is important. As an employer, that means that showing employees how their individual contributions tie into the larger purpose of the organization is highly valued. It's motivating for the entire team.

Hospitality is also a big part of Indian culture, and people there go to great lengths to take care of guests. For example, they'll pick guests up at the airport, check them in at the hotel, get them a hot beverage—they are caretakers, which contrasts sometimes starkly to the independent American culture that takes great pride in doing things on their own.

After recognizing the lengths to which our Indian team members went in order to care for their visitors, Globalization Partners hired a cultural leader at our Boston headquarters office whose sole responsibility is to provide hospitality to our international guests. It's her job to pick up our guests at the airport, take them to their hotel room, pick them up at the hotel in the morning to walk them to the office, introduce them to people in the office, and take them out to lunch and dinner—it's a whole program. The program was developed after experiencing truly exceptional levels of hospitality from our Indian and Mexican colleagues, in particular. The idea of letting people land in an airport and figure things out is a very American way of letting your international team show up at HQ. We realized we had much to learn by importing our Indian and Mexico team's hospitality traditions. Besides building stronger cultural ties to our local team members when they visit HQ, it's also brought a lot of fun and joy to our team.

Because Indian culture places importance on caring for others, as an employer, it's appreciated when you ask about an employee's family—expressing interest in the people who are important to them and getting to know what they do outside of work. Due to India's traditions, locals may find it strange if a man asked another man about his wife, however, so it might be better to ask about family in general or children, and let the employee pick up the topic from there.

India is also more formal and hierarchical. In the "old days," when we all Zoomed in from office locations, if we asked our India team to speak to the group, they would always defer to their leader, who would speak on behalf of the local office team. People are more likely to look for instruction from the top, as compared to American colleagues, who are taught a less hierarchal and less formal management structure—especially in technology companies.

COMMUNICATION STYLE

Where Americans aim to be direct in their communications, Indians are typically more comfortable with indirect language, especially when they fear disappointing you. So, you really need to listen carefully for the underlying message, especially when you aren't hearing a direct, "Yes, that can be done."

When something can't be done, you're more likely to hear, "We'll try our best," or "We'll see," or "Hmm, possibly." It's likely the answer you're being given is "no," but no one wants to be so bold as to come right out and say that to you. Saying "no" directly would be rude.

They also like to discuss important matters in person, rather than by email or phone. During those meetings, it's useful to watch body language. Indians often move their heads from side to side (with ears moving toward each shoulder rather than rotating left and right) as if they are weighing options. This generally means, "I understand your words," but it does not mean yes or no. A Zoom call is much better than audio-only for international work, and we highly recommend having a policy of video on all the time during calls.

Fifty-five percent of communication is nonverbal, according to research by Professor Albert Mehrabian.[19] In the digital workforce, having video on all the time is a must-have for international management. If 55 percent of communication is nonverbal between common language speakers, it must be higher when people are speaking a foreign language. In addition, being able to see your face and read your body language and, indeed, read your lips, is important when employees are listening carefully to a speaker in a foreign language. While most of the people that we hire on behalf of our customers speak English, which is considered the international business language, it's important to remember that it is a second language for most people in the world, not first, and nuance is incredibly important. Video on makes remote work, work.

Indians are typically not as comfortable with physical touch in business, so the occasional American hug between close colleagues is generally uncomfortable and is certainly not done between men and women. A handshake is normal or putting your hands together in a prayerful "namaste" gesture with a warm verbal greeting. Don't hug or kiss your colleagues in India unless they grew up in America and they initiate first.

COST STRUCTURE AND TALENT RETENTION

Historically, in comparison to talent in other countries, India's salaries have been much lower. That meant that hiring managers had greater access to skilled workers at lower wages than in other parts of the world. That made companies want to hire employees in droves. Why not, when you can hire competent accountants for one-sixth of what you'd pay in America?

It makes perfect sense. However, since 2020 we have seen salaries in India increase dramatically, especially in more senior IT roles.

Although wages may be lower than in other countries, the management, communication, and time zone issues can make it hard to train and retain talent. Related to that, it is customary for Indian employees to receive a review, and a corresponding increase of 7 to 10 percent every year. Most often, expect a title change every year or every other year—and by customary, I mean borderline mandatory, if you want to hold onto your employees. Indian professionals are under incredible pressure to be promoted at work. The reason, if you can imagine, is that when someone makes only US$5,000 per year, for example, moving jobs for an additional US$500 per year actually makes sense. This drives CFOs crazy—the idea that someone would quit their job for US$500 a year is terrible for a business. Companies unwilling to have a constant promotion cycle or recognize high-performing employees are likely to have trouble retaining their best people. Job hopping is common in India, especially in the technology sector, because just like everyone, everywhere, they want the best for their families—and that requires regular increases and promotions.

It's important to note that no one ever wants to be considered "cheap talent." Never treat your employees, or anyone, like their work is worth less simply because the cost structure in their country may be less than it is in the U.S. While that cost structure is attractive, treating people with the dignity and potential that they deserve is critical to your success, and everyone else's. That's the way to build a winning team.

If you want your India office to be successful, you have to play the game according to local terms. We recommend taking great care and investing the time required for your India team. We've found some of our most extraordinary talent in India, and what they bring to the table is truly exceptional. We also have very high retention rates, which I attribute to the strength of our local leadership and our willingness to listen to our local advisors about what's important in-market.

SEQUOIA CONSULTING GROUP

Sequoia Consulting Group is a tech-enabled consulting and services company that provides benefits, human resources, payroll, and risk management solutions for people-centric employers with 20 to 20,000 people. The Sequoia People Platform centralizes workforce data and helps companies navigate complex issues so they can maximize their investment in people, whether they are in-office, distributed, or global. For two decades, Sequoia has been working with companies to balance the needs of their businesses with the needs of their people.

Sequoia has approximately 450 employees, with offices in the San Francisco Bay Area, New York, Tempe, and Bangalore. As of February 2021, most of its team members were working remotely to comply with state and regional stay-at-home orders. Because of those orders, the firm is now more open to hiring outside of its traditional talent markets, near its offices, though, globally, its hiring is still focused on Bangalore.

In response to pandemic-related restrictions, the firm has learned new ways to collaborate with its tools, as well as learning new capabilities for recruiting, hiring, and onboarding people. Sequoia developed new internal communication processes and methods to keep people connected and invested in new well-being vendors and services to better take care of its people.

Sequoia provides consulting services across a broad spectrum of business needs. Many of its clients engage the firm to support their U.S. employee benefit programs, global consulting, and risk and retirement wealth accumulation. Those clients range from startups to well-established multinationals with expansive global footprints. Pre-pandemic, most of Sequoia's clients were already comfortable with digital hiring, communicating with employees through a number of methods and work-from-home policies.

Most of those clients are already operating as multinationals; growth continues to be prevalent outside of the U.S., with a focus on global business centers of influence. Clients are primarily growing outside of their home counties to better meet and understand the needs of their customers, create a diverse business community, and be at the leading edge of attracting talent in developing markets. Globalization Partners acts as an adjunct to Sequoia customers, enabling the same high-value service they provide to their customers in America to extend beyond U.S. borders.

TERMS OF EMPLOYMENT CONTRACTS

Since Indian labor law is very complex, it's important to spell out in great detail all the elements of an employment agreement. At a minimum, the annual compensation, benefits, and termination clauses—reasons for termination—should be clearly addressed.

Employees in India are typically concerned with more than just their salary. In fact, there are many allowances that employees will request that can add up to as much as 60 percent of their total benefits package, which ultimately reduce the total tax bill to the employee. It's complicated. For that reason, we often recommend negotiating a "total cost of compensation" as a gross amount, which includes everything the employee will receive. Then, let the employee navigate the details of how that is structured via the local accounting and payroll team (or via your Employer of Record) so that both parties can structure it in a way that makes sense.

In addition to pay, Indian employees place an extremely high value on job titles that suggest responsibility and prestige. Among professionals in India, having a prestigious title is important. In some cases, even a higher salary can't compensate for what is perceived as a weak title.

At the same time, there are drawbacks to granting lofty titles. Because great respect and stature accompany such designations, certain work may be viewed as beneath the station of a director-level employee, for example. While director-level employees in the U.S. are generally more flexible and willing to complete tasks or projects at all levels to ensure their company is well supported, Indian directors may hesitate to do certain things they consider a risk to their high-level status. Overly titled employees may also demand a support staff befitting their rank. Negotiating such situations can be tricky, and it's wise, as it is anywhere, to take the full situation into account with the support of a local advisor.

Time Off

The standard Indian workweek is 40 hours of five eight-hour days, but it should not exceed 50 hours total, or nine hours a day.

The minimum number of vacation days that employees receive per year is 21 days, but senior managers and executives may request more.

Employees must receive seven sick days, and pregnant women and new mothers are entitled to 26 weeks of maternity leave. Maternity leave can start up to eight weeks before the due date and the remaining weeks used after the child is born. With each child, the employee receives INR₹3,500 (about US$50) as a medical bonus. If the employee is a factory worker, the government pays the bonus; otherwise, the employer is responsible.

Termination

Terminating employees for reasons other than cause can get costly, so it is recommended that new employees be given a three-month probationary period, which is typical. Employers also have the option to add an additional three months.

Employers or employees must give 30 days' notice of intent to sever the employment agreement in writing; during the probationary period the minimum is 15 days. However, the employer does have the option to make a payment to the employee instead of providing sufficient notice.

Employees who are let go for reasons unrelated to performance are generally entitled to 15 days of pay for each year of employment. Those who have been employed for five or more years are also entitled to a gratuity payment, which is calculated as the annual base salary plus Dearness Allowance, multiplied by 15/26 multiplied by years of service.

INFRASTRUCTURE

One of the biggest challenges of doing business in India can be the unreliable infrastructure, including high-speed internet service and electricity. For example, office parks in Bangalore have high-speed internet, but the infrastructure of the country is challenging in that sometimes entire cities get flooded, such as Delhi only a few years ago. Besides affecting the office Wi-Fi, this can have a significant impact on your employees' lives. We mostly hire team members in large cities and have not had any trouble in recent years. The infrastructure issues are being addressed, and things are generally reliable enough in the large cities.

Due to this, India also never went fully remote the way the U.S. did during the pandemic. Employees may need to go to the office to work because their homes are often not set up for work from home due to the space and equipment required. This does not mean everyone, of course, and it's worth discussing this with your local team and potential hires as they come on board. India, like everywhere else, is facing a changing landscape since the pandemic, and individual circumstances vary a lot.

Although the business landscape in India continues to evolve and grow, it may not always be in sync with the general pace of change you are accustomed to. There is a lot of red tape involved in getting things done, so make sure to take that into account when putting together your business plan. Things can be frustrating, hard to figure out, and sometimes local ways of doing things won't make much sense to outsiders.

Things are stable, but India just has its own pace that works for them. So you need to be willing to adapt and adjust your timeline accordingly.

ADDITIONAL RESOURCES

For more information about the realities of doing business in India, turn to the following resources: globaltalentunleashed. com/chapter-6

CHAPTER 7

Doing Business in Europe

Europe is a top consideration for many companies looking to hire global teams, partly due to the size of the market—many companies see expanding into Europe as a good way to add a huge market opportunity. There's also a great, highly educated, and multilingual talent pool.

In general, Europe is the first landing place where U.S. companies set up sales and marketing teams outside North America. A typical structure is a VP of sales in London, with sales and growth teams in the Netherlands, Germany, France, and elsewhere, and a consolidated back office in a lower-cost jurisdiction with a large multilingual talent pool.

Companies also like to hire logistics and engineering teams in Europe due to the proximity to the East Coast of the U.S. and the abundant talent. Finally, North American companies love Europe because there is a level of comfort and familiarity with that part of the world that makes it appealing. European work habits are similar to American habits in some ways that are comforting to Americans, although that's not to downplay the cultural differences, which must also be taken into account.

While some European countries do provide a lower labor cost structure on paper, that is not true everywhere; Europe consists of more than 40 countries, each with its own culture, laws, expectations, and economy. Much like the U.S., there are industry clusters in different parts of Europe just as, say, Silicon Valley is known for tech and venture capital, New York City is known for finance, and Austin is known for startups. The Ile-de-France region is one of the top R&D and engineering clusters, for example. Beyond that, social insurance costs, employee protections, and some of the terms of doing business can be a surprise if you're not expecting them. Those also vary significantly and are different in all European countries.

But before you start making plans to set up a hub in Europe, there are a few things to understand about the region.

CULTURE

One of the biggest cultural differences between the U.S. and Europe is the importance of work in our lives. In the U.S., almost everything revolves around work—it's at the center of our identities, it's how we spend the majority of our days, and it takes up a good portion of mental energy, even when we're home. U.S. employees often take pride in the long hours they work, or the lengths to which they are willing to go to exceed expectations in their roles. Evenings and weekends are often spent at work, and in many cases, promotion opportunities go to those who are willing to put in the extra hours. Although the standard workweek is 40 hours—and that is what salaries are based on—there are no restrictions on how many hours per week employees can spend in the office in the U.S. In some firms, 50, 60, or even 80 hours can be expected.

Almost the opposite is the case in Europe, where employees are protected from having to work much beyond a 40-hour week. Although the laws vary from country to country, most prohibit companies from requiring employees to work more than 48 hours per week. Companies doing business in Europe are also required to give much more paid time off than in the U.S.—and your employees will take their time off, unlike their American counterparts.

With trends and fads in Europe not always in sync with America, it is quite possible that products that aren't selling as well as expected in the U.S. could do very well in Europe. Test marketing is key to understand the dynamic, but many companies discover that expanding into Europe gives their products and services new life. And with over 743 million people residing in Europe, it's a sizeable potential market.[20]

HYDROLIX

Although Hydrolix is headquartered in Portland, Oregon, fewer than half of its 23 employees are based there. The company develops database software for companies all around the world, and, for that reason, its team stretches across 14 U.S. cities and three continents.

Hydrolix hired its first international employee, Jason, within six months of opening its doors. Jason had worked alongside one of Hydrolix's co-founders at two other companies and was at the top of their list for international talent; he is based in the UK, just outside of London.

Jason was an essential addition to the company's talent pool. During the early development phase of the company, he was the only customer-facing employee. Now, as the business has started to scale-out its global sales, services, and support functions, all new employees are being trained directly by Jason.

Given the paperwork required to establish a UK subsidiary, it's unlikely Hydrolix would have invested the time and effort just for the sake of one employee, but thanks to Globalization Partners, bringing Jason onboard involved none of the standard administrative hassles. Since then, Hydrolix has hired employees in Canada, Spain, India, Israel, Thailand, and Vietnam.

Although the pandemic forced Hydrolix to temporarily close its physical offices, all employees continue to use the same tools, participate in the same meetings, and interact as usual online. It's likely the company will remain a globally distributed business well into the future.

One of the big benefits of having a globally distributed business is that customers, to their surprise sometimes, are supported during their local business hours anywhere in the world and receive 24/7 on-call support from the Hydrolix team, thanks to its global presence.

It's now possible, via Globalization Partners' global employment platform, to leverage an international talent pool without having to deal directly with a ton of complex regulations. Globalization Partners lets Hydrolix focus on building out its team without having to worry about the administrative details.

Communication Style

Although many people in the European workforce speak English, it is not the official language outside the UK and Ireland. English is merely one of the 23 working languages of the European Union. Over 60 percent of the populations in Sweden, Denmark, Finland, Austria, and the Netherlands do speak English, however.

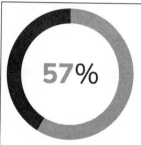

57 percent of people in France are reasonably proficient in English. In Paris, that percentage is a bit higher at just over 60 percent.

Source: www.thelocal.fr

Many professionals are comfortable with the direct communication style Americans generally present, though they may not be quite as direct themselves. In my experience running a cross-border team, the cultural gaps are most likely to surface when people don't realize that minor communication differences are related to cultural norms. For example, Americans value the concept of getting immediately to work, being efficient with time, and directing team members with follow-up action items. Europeans sometimes take offense at this "all business" style on Zoom call after Zoom call since, culturally, they focus more on relationships, and generally spend more time getting to consensus and with a bit of small talk before launching into business. This builds trust and confidence between professional contacts.

Europeans are significantly less direct in their communication style. As an American working internationally, I have trained myself to open email communication with overseas team members by asking how the team member is, commenting on something unrelated to our work or about the world at large, and greeting the team member warmly before jumping into my question or comment related to work. I learned this by witnessing the offense taken by European colleagues who often don't understand why their American colleagues are being so "rude," when no offense was intended by the person speaking or running the meeting. As an American, my natural tendency is to just get straight to work, so I had to adjust my habits.

STRUCTURING AND LAWS: THERE IS NO PAN-EUROPEAN OPTION

The European Union is an economic alliance, mostly united by a common currency, the free movement of labor, goods, services and financial capital, and a commitment to working together as a block. It is NOT united by a pan-European tax or employment law system. Each country in Europe is indeed different. In any country where you hire employees, or do any activity that triggers a corporate taxable presence, you would normally need to set up a different legal entity and follow the unique labor laws of that country.

In sum, there is no one "pan-European" structure that you can set up, and every country is different in terms of labor law, tax requirements, and business law. This makes a good Employer of Record even more important because your competent EOR will have to set up the legal infrastructure that makes sense for each country.

Cost Structure

Depending on the particular country, labor costs may be lower, the same, or higher than typical U.S. compensation and benefits packages. Some of that difference is due to location, with major cities generally paying higher salaries to be in line with higher costs of living there. The British pound is fairly expensive, but labor costs are generally lower outside London; and in France, the typical cost of social security contributions for employers on top of labor amount to approximately 45–49 percent of an employee's gross salary. In Romania, costs to hire people are generally significantly less. However, this is changing quickly with the digitization of the global workforce.

Typically, if you can set up shop in a suburban or more rural locale, the cost of your labor should be lower than a city location. And if part of your expansion into Europe is to be able to manufacture products closer to your customers, it may cost you less to manufacture your products there rather shipping them in finished form over the Atlantic; that gets expensive quickly.

The European Union is an economic alliance, mostly united by a common currency, the free movement of labor, and a commitment to working together as a block. It is not united by a common tax or employment law system.

EMPLOYMENT CONTRACTS

There are some European countries where protection of employees from on-the-job exploitation, as is most evident in France, can lead to employment contracts that are seen as extremely pro-employee by international standards. That means that the employment land-scape is highly regulated; that there are limits on what employees can be asked to do. Firing employees is complicated and difficult, even with a contract in place. A locally compliant employment contract is usually legally required in the local language and is also one of your best sources of protection in case anything goes sideways. My best advice is to make sure your employment contract is tight (whether provided by your in-house legal team or via an Employer of Record) and to follow all the nuanced laws carefully.

Beyond the terms of the contract, European employees usually know their rights and are more likely than employees elsewhere to use the threat of a lawsuit as leverage with an employer. In many countries, the employees have free access to labor tribunals. Employers generally realize it's easier to settle, and often do. The most common mistake we see international companies make in Europe is expecting that they can terminate or treat employees in Europe the same way they treat American employees, with terms such as at-will employment.

In an attempt to circumvent this situation, some companies hire independent contractors to get work done on an as-needed basis. For that reason, more governments are cracking down on such arrangements, looking closely at companies that retain freelancers, or independent contractors. If such workers are found to have a working relationship closer to that of an employee, the employer can be hit with sizeable fines and penalties, as well as be held responsible for never having declared that it was doing business in the country or that it had local employees. Having a locally compliant contract in place is your best means of protection.

Serbia, Poland, Hungary, and Romania, in particular, have clarified laws recently to make it even more evident who is a true contractor, with multiple customers, and who is actually an employee, with one customer and strict guidelines about where and when work will be done.

REAL IMPACT GLOBAL B.V.

Real Impact Global B.V. is a global technology-driven impact project execution company operating from its headquarters in the Hague, Netherlands, and a special-purpose company in Switzerland. The company focuses on engaging high-impact projects and implementing them as fast as possible at the lowest risk to everyone concerned, in order to implement real solutions for some of the world's biggest challenges. Recently, these challenges also became major global risks requiring urgent action.

Real Impact Global partnered with Globalization Partners because of our unique business model and offering. Although Real Impact Global is an early-stage technology company, intentionally implementing a global operating structure, its model is challenging traditional definitions of growth and value. Its growth is fast, and its key value as a business is to humanity.

For the first time in history, technology makes it possible to implement with speed and at scale. During its first-phase implementation, it hired operational teams in 18 countries across Africa, Asia, and Latin America. The biggest challenge was to get business process, technology, and people aligned to its operating model, which was critical to ensuring it could identify, engage, and implement high-impact projects across the world.

Real Impact Global did not merely plan to go global over time; its business and operating model were designed as a global project execution model, meaning it was essential to implement the global operating structure from the beginning. The operating model was designed to have autonomous, self-directed teams working remotely all over the world. Globalization Partners was a perfect partner to help Real Impact Global with this process because we enabled the company to hire and manage international team members without having to set up complex infrastructure.

The Covid-19 pandemic had an incredible impact on health services worldwide with major economic repercussions. The full economic fallout of the pandemic is yet to be determined, but as it unfolds, industries are decimated, and millions of paid working hours have been lost to employees across the world. An estimated 150 million people will be pushed back into extreme poverty, putting human progress made over the last 20 years at risk. Economies were already under pressure prior to the pandemic, and it will likely take years for countries to get back to pre-pandemic economic levels. This global crisis has changed the world as we know it, and as it plays out, we must push forward and ensure that we engage with the issues at hand. Real Impact Global has been working on a solution that is now required at a global level to implement at scale and speed.

Speedy implementations obviously hold challenges, but the company quickly identified the short- and long-term implications and impact on the business. The first impact was the realization of workarounds that would be necessary to cope with the new normal.

That meant increasing the remote working percentage of its entire staff. Covid forced Real Impact Global to implement even faster because of its mission and purpose. It forced management to move some of its strategic components earlier and to review its infrastructure requirements—all of which had a positive impact.

The only negative of remote working was that, at face value, it seemed to compromise team culture and team engagement. The current challenge is figuring out how to continue with remote working, leveraging the advantages while also developing a strong organizational and team culture.

TIME OFF

Many countries in Europe are very protective of their residents, placing limits on how much they can be expected to work in a week. Hence, the 48-hour-per-week maximum work length. In addition, some countries shut down for entire months of holiday during the summer, which employers must deal with. For example, in Sweden, one payroll company we know of shuts down its office and goes on vacation for the entire month of August. They run payroll for all their customers a month in advance and don't accept any changes. This is considered normal in Sweden.

TERMINATION

One business area that is considerably different from the U.S. includes European labor laws surrounding termination—it can be more difficult to terminate employees in Europe. That's not to say it's impossible, but you should expect it will take much longer and cost much more to take someone off your payroll. In some countries, it's illegal to terminate a person without specific and well-defined cause. When this situation arises, what usually happens from a practical perspective is that both parties agree to some severance and mutually agree to terminate the contract. In any situation related to a termination in Europe, good legal and human resources support is a wise investment.

INFRASTRUCTURE

Except in small, remote villages, the European infrastructure is well-established, stable, and strong. Electricity, internet service, and Wi-Fi are readily available in nearly every city.

As labor shortages grow worldwide, several European cities are becoming tech hubs that are attracting employers and employees alike. Some of the hottest cities now, according to Savills Tech Cities, are:

- Amsterdam

- Barcelona

- Berlin

- Copenhagen

- Dublin

- London

- Stockholm

Due to the large number of countries in one geographic region, Europe may be a little harder to navigate in terms of rules and regulations, but remains an excellent starting point for hiring a global team. Exactly where you want to hire will depend on what you want people to do.

Additional Resources

For more information about the realities of doing business in Europe, turn to the following resources: globaltalentunleashed. com/chapter-7

CHAPTER 8

Asia-Pacific, the Region
That's Immune to Recession

Asia is a vast landscape and provides enough opportunity to fill a book of its own. Rather than try to articulate everything in this brief chapter, we'll focus on the core locations for hiring and market expansion that our North American and European customers focus on: Singapore, Australia, Japan, China, Hong Kong, Malaysia, the Philippines, Thailand, and Vietnam.

There are a number of factors that have contributed, and continue to contribute, to the Asian region's resilience and the emerging business opportunities here. One of the biggest is the favorable demographics and its educated global workforce. Another is the existence of free-trade agreements designed to foster more in-region business dealings, such as the Comprehensive and Progressive Agreement for Trans-Pacific Partnership (CPTPP) and the Regional Comprehensive Economic Partnership (RCEP). As a result of these partnerships, the Association of Southeast Asian Nations (ASEAN) region is now the world's biggest free-trade pact, covering a market of 2.2 billion people.[21] However, perhaps the biggest contributor to the region's continued resilience in the face of disease (SARS, Avian flu, Swine flu, etc.), financial crisis in the late 1990s, regime changes, and being at the epicenter of Covid-19, has been the population's focus on the greater good. Placing society's best interests as a top priority makes it possible to bounce back faster from challenges and conflicts.

Due to the rapid influx of venture capital, private equity, and several large mergers and acquisitions, the vibrant market opportunity and talent pools, and the now startup-friendly region, global companies are eager to do business in this dynamic, fast-growing part of the world. Google, Microsoft, Amazon, Facebook, Hewlett-Packard, IBM, and Intel are well-established in the region, serving to attract new names that want to follow in their footsteps.

The market potential of Asia is massive; the region is the third-largest market in the world and home to 60 percent of the world's population. When we at Globalization Partners created our own business plans, we assumed the economic potential we perceive in North America could be doubled if we added Europe or tripled if we added both Europe and Asia. That's a common metric used by high-growth software companies.

WHY TO GO AND HOW TO STRUCTURE

Many of our North American and European customers expand into Asia in order to tackle the huge market opportunity. A typical structure for this would be to hire a VP of sales, Asia, based out of Singapore or Hong Kong—Singapore has become increasingly common in the last few years, as has Australia. The VP of sales would typically hire a small team in Singapore for strategic work, perhaps a small sales team, a head of demand generation for Asia, and a few other critical hires. Thereafter, the VP would typically hire one or two salespeople in multiple countries, spanning Korea, Hong Kong, key cities in China, Sydney, and Bangkok. The VP would also hire a strong general manager (GM) for Japan if the company decides to tackle the Japanese market.

Some companies also supplement their strategic sales team with operational hubs for lower-cost, back-office talent throughout Asia-Pacific, including Visa, Barclay's Bank, Accenture, and H&M. Malaysia is one country known for its multilingual, talented workforce. The Philippines is known for excellent back-office customer service and marketing support. India remains a back-office hub for much of the world, so much so that we included it in a separate chapter. For manufacturing, China is the mecca of the world, as well as a huge market in its own right, and an innovation hub. Vietnam and Indonesia are gaining traction fast as new manufacturing hubs.

Why do most companies hire another GM in Japan, People's Republic of China (PR China), or Korea if they already have a senior sales VP in Singapore? Companies are most successful when they localize, setting up talent and leadership in a local market. If you're going to tackle the ASEAN market, hire a strong local GM from a similar industry with established industry ties. This is incredibly important, because your local GM says *everything* about who your company is and how successful you will be in the local market. You need someone with established relationships who understands the market. He or she will also need to build the local team, which would be very hard if you didn't have the right GM.

In Japan, it's particularly hard for international companies to hire GMs, or anyone, because, culturally, the brand name of the company an individual works for is really important. People don't want to work for a startup that no one has ever heard of. In Japan, that includes the hottest companies in the Silicon Valley. Much to the dismay of some of our highest-growth customers, the prestige you've garnered in the Bay Area and in tech hubs globally might not help you at all in Japan. Prestige and security come from working with Mitsubishi, and entrepreneurship doesn't have the sex appeal in Japan that it does elsewhere. When they do exist, the good bilingual and bicultural GMs are snapped up by Bitcoin, LinkedIn, and other extremely well-known name brands. In sum, most international companies have a very hard time competing for talent in Japan, especially for that critical top hire.

Besides the difficulty of establishing the right talent to really take over the market, it takes a long time for even a successful GM to crack the Japanese market. We were recently advised to assume it would take 10 years for one of our key customers to really gain traction in Japan. That said, we've seen companies do it, including Netsuite, which was one of my earliest and most successful customers in Japan. If you're going to go into Japan, go big, find the right talent, localize your entire company to be effective in-market, and don't expect a fast ROI. But don't let those words daunt you if you're planning to conquer the globe; journeys of a thousand miles begin with a single step. Just know it's going to take a while, and build that into your business plan.

Beyond its huge size and the variety of options, there are some important things to understand about the vast territory of Asia before you jump in.

CULTURE

In Northeast Asian culture, there is also a focus on relationships. It can be more difficult to solidify contracts or confirm deals until and unless a personal relationship is established there. Getting to know the people you're doing business with on a personal level is essential to being successful in this part of Asia. It's also the first step toward building trust. Who you know matters a lot in Asian countries.

HIRE LOCALS: A RECIPE FOR SUCCESS

Many North American companies love the comfort of having an American go to Asia to establish their sales channel. They're comfortable with the individual chosen and know that person wants to go and will work hard. Maybe they'll learn the language with time. However, exporting an American to sell into Asia without the intention of having him or her hire and train locals is a recipe for failure. The employee might mean well, but the individual is literally starting from scratch, in terms of language, culture, and relationships.

While it can seem intimidating to start a search for local talent in a completely unfamiliar country, it's much better to do the hard work upfront. Find a rock star locally, and let him or her build a team. Hiring local is the recipe for success.

The younger generation of workers entering the workforce is vastly different from previous generations. They want more freedom and less hierarchy, and are infinitely more technologically savvy, far beyond their peers or colleagues in the West.

The demand for increased choice and mobility/remote work among those in the Asia-Pacific region has emerged in recent years. In Japan, younger people are unaware of the once-prominent corporate employee who was fiercely devoted to his or her employer. This helps explain the difference in work attitudes between older people in Japan, who were brought up to believe private time should be sacrificed for the good of the company, and the young, who place more importance on achieving a work-life balance. Across Asia-Pacific, the youth of the population (particularly in markets such as Indonesia and the Philippines), is a key differentiator compared with other parts of the world. These younger populations have already been and will continue to push the boundaries of how mobility and technology can impact every facet of their lives. Examples of how technology and remote work, as well as the burgeoning middle class, are disrupting old stereotypes related to the hierarchical "Asian culture" are popping up all over. Look at the People's Republic of China, where many wealthy Chinese are acquiring offshore assets, property, and bank accounts while sending their children to Western universities. Or look at the ubiquity of access to mobile internet and how AI has infused the design of nearly every facet of daily life. These shifts are rippling through the culture and serving to completely rewrite the traditional views of how the many cultures of the region operate.

COMMUNICATION STYLE

Communication in Asian culture is generally indirect, requiring U.S. managers to develop an ability to read between the lines, to understand the message that is actually being conveyed. However, this is less true in Australia and New Zealand, which are part of the region but more direct in their communication style.

Similar to the culture in India, certain cultures in East Asia consider it impolite to say "no" to a request directly. Instead, you'll often hear a pause and then something like, "Hmm, we may be able to get it done," or "It's possible . . ." Americans might hear those responses as, "Yes, we can get it done, perhaps with some additional resources or time," but what the respondent is often trying to convey is, "No, it can't be done."

It's important for Americans to listen carefully for the subtle "no" they may not be hearing. Try to recognize that many workers would much rather be polite, especially if you are their superior, and not get the job done as you expect than to be rude and tell you "no" upfront. It just won't happen.

If you try and get clarity by asking follow-up questions, especially by email, and are met with silence, your "no" has been confirmed. The employee believes he or she has said "no" several times and it would only be ruder to keep saying no. The non-communication is another way of conveying this. Of course, an employee not responding to email is the ultimate deal-breaker for an American, and so this communication and cultural gap between East and West has caused more work-relationship issues than we can count.

However, this avoidance of the word "no" is not the case throughout the whole region. Although people in East Asia tend to be less assertive and forthcoming than South Asians, South Asians actually encourage assertiveness and debate in interpersonal communication.

Reading up on cross-cultural communication styles and learning to listen for "no" is valuable.

ECOLEX

Established in 2005, Ecolex is a dedicated producer of vegetable oil-based products for home and personal care products, animal feeds, and food emulsifiers. Based in Singapore, Ecolex was looking to hire talent outside of its home market in the U.S. When evaluating options, it found providers, but each was limited to payroll processing, accounting, and tax services—there was no single solution that covered all of Ecolex's needs. It also prioritized looking for a partner that would stay on top of changing, complex international regulations.

"Not only is it costly to assimilate to local tax laws, the U.S. framework is extremely complex, while Japan has another set of rules. I'd rather leave it to experts than dedicate our own resources to a resource- and time-consuming task," says Rosalind Lee, Corporate Finance and Business Controller at Ecolex.

Finding the right service provider is not as easy as it sounds, however. A global expansion partner should be zealous in respecting international labor law, experienced in compliance, and quick on their feet.

"Working with our previous provider was difficult because of the time difference. It was a U.S.-based company, whereas we are in Singapore. But we couldn't do it alone, and processing payroll in a timely manner, meeting all the statutory requirements at local and federal levels, and ensuring compliance with the Employment Pass (EP) for our American talent was paramount," Lee explains.

Ecolex decided to team up with an efficient ally, relying on Globalization Partners' global employment platform to bypass growing pains. This partnership enabled the company to quickly expand to other markets for product testing prior to entity setup. "Going to an EOR (Employer of Record) is definitely the best choice at a company's early growth stage. As your business scales, hiring via an EOR means you can continue to grow seamlessly until reaching the critical mass that justifies setting up a legal entity," Lee says.

One of Globalization Partners' main advantages is a local presence with a global reach. Ecolex gained access to a full-service platform that bypasses the need for third-party advice and provides a one-stop shop global growth solution. By relying on Globalization Partners' stream-lined international growth platform, companies such as Ecolex can focus time and resources on what they do best: growing their business.

"We are now able to focus our efforts on the Chinese market to significantly improve our margins by going directly to the end cus-tomer instead of relying on a local distributor. By unlocking a local presence, we can provide a more specialized, technical offering to our customers that a distributor cannot," Lee explains.

The Ecolex team is now confident expanding wherever it detects demand. In fact, the company plans to use Globalization Partners' platform as a pivotal component in the next step of its growth plans— consolidating teams in Argentina. Ecolex unlocked the ability to seamlessly integrate teams of local talent—an invaluable advantage when it comes to consolidating a local footprint in a new market and taking business to new heights.

EMPLOYMENT CONTRACTS AND TERMS

Although many states in the U.S. have "at-will employment," meaning that employer or employee can decide to end the relationship for any reason at any time, this concept is practically unheard of in some countries in Asia. Employer/employee relationships are still expected to last almost one's entire life, although that's changing. In any case, most Asian countries do not require the same detailed employment contracts that European companies require. Nevertheless, an employment contract is often the best way to protect yourself.

There are a few customs that employers should be aware of before hiring in Asia. One is that of a 13th-month bonus pay, which is mandatory in some countries, such as Indonesia and the Philippines, and expected, or considered a best practice, in other countries. The 13th-month payment is an extra month of pay given either at the end of the year or during a holiday. It's a bonus that is almost inevitably expected. We notice that some of our customers are confused by this, and indeed, end up offering a greater annual salary than they had intended by multiplying the offered monthly salary by 12 instead of 13. Be clear when you offer a salary to an employee in Asia as to whether it includes the 13th-month bonus (or not).

WINSHUTTLE

Over 2,400 enterprises globally trust Winshuttle's process automation, product information management (PIM), and multi-domain master data management (MDM) software to drive business results at scale, become more agile, and transform digital into a competitive advantage.

Winshuttle believed it was crucial to have a global team so that the company could relate to all of its customers wherever they are located. Having a geographically dispersed team enables Winshuttle to provide localized solution support to help solve its customers' most critical, unique business problems. Having a more diverse team helps Winshuttle continuously improve and grow with a true global perspective.

The company recognized the benefits of having a global team nearly 17 years ago, when it first expanded outside of the U.S. However, in the early years of the expansion, the company also experienced firsthand the challenges associated with having team members scattered around the world when it tried to set it up in-house without Globalization Partners' support, including navigating local labor laws, understanding local business customs, and supporting team members through language barriers, among other key tasks.

Globalization Partners has helped Winshuttle spread its footprint and company culture across borders, enjoying all the benefits of being a global organization without the logistical difficulties traditionally associated with having a dispersed team.

The company also has the added benefit of being able to test new territories that would otherwise be too difficult to hire in by putting resources behind one new team member before expanding more quickly and widely, should the location prove to be promising. At the same time, Winshuttle employees abroad benefit from having local experts who can understand and help resolve their unique HR needs, with the opportunity to work for a rapidly expanding, innovative employer regardless of where they live.

Winshuttle is based in the U.S. with headquarters in Bothell, Washington. Today, the company has more than 350 team members across 10 countries, including the U.S., UK, France, Germany, India, Singapore, Spain, Sweden, Australia, and Canada.

Via Globalization Partners, Winshuttle intends to continue expanding and further diversifying its team so that it can continue to support organizations worldwide with their digital transformation initiatives.

TERMINATION

The concept of "saving face" or preserving dignity runs deep in Asia, even in situations when an employee is being let go for poor performance. When an employee is not performing, for whatever reason, it is essential that the process of ending the relationship be handled respectfully. This is true in all cultures, that termination should be handled respectfully, but especially so in this region. That means expressing gratitude for the employee's many contributions to the company's success. The employee, regardless of culture or location, needs to feel respected and cared for. Then, the suggestion can be made that while the individual's skills are impressive, the company's needs have shifted and another organization would certainly be better able to make full use of those abilities.

In some places, like Singapore and Hong Kong, the termination notice and communication are fairly straightforward. In other countries with more complicated termination procedures, this conversation is something of a dance, balancing respect and graciousness with the need to convey that the employee should look for another job. In that type of circumstance, it is more typical that the employment relationship is ended by mutual agreement, with a severance package arranged for the valued employee so that the employee can move forward in his or her career and the relationship can be preserved for all involved.

In general, we believe that facilitating a graceful exit is best practice for everyone, everywhere. However, in Asia, showing respect for people is even more critical due to the concept of saving face. It is also important for managing the rest of the team after the individual's departure.

INFRASTRUCTURE

East Asia and the Southeast Asian region have come a long way in a very short amount of time in regard to its work infrastructure. Due to the influx of investment and young population—more than half of its residents are under 30 years old—Southeast Asia is a leading mobile-first market known for developing and adopting leading-edge technology. Today, in fact, 90 percent of internet users go online using their mobile phones. Some island nations do have less reliable infrastructure than others, but we have not found any of these issues to be insurmountable in the places where companies commonly hire large teams.

There is now an incredible opportunity to harness the economic engine of the Asia-Pacific region. The powerful demographic pivot toward youth, as well as a well-educated, technologically savvy talent pool, is set to deliver on the decades-old promise of the Asian Century. The result is building excitement within a region that is changing and leaping ahead of old, tired, 20th century "how to do business in Asia" stereotypes. The youthful talent here today is looking for meaning and purpose first and foremost. Across Asia-Pacific, the traditional cultural values of contributing to the greater good are now coinciding with global trends among the younger generation.

There are three ways the Asia-Pacific workplace is being affected by this broader global shift:

1. People are gravitating toward opportunities that match their need for meaning.

2. Companies are now adapting their organizational goals to reflect the increasing need for meaning. In this post-pandemic

world, that means revisiting their values to ensure they align with the new world in which we are operating.

3. While adapting to people's needs to contribute to meaningful work, companies must focus on their employees' well-being, particularly given the remote nature of our work, the rapid changes taking place in the region, and the tendency to experience burnout.

The vast majority of people in the Asia-Pacific region are excited about being able to do work that is personally meaningful. Most are also excited about the ability to search for work at organizations that show a commitment to the well-being of their employees. Companies that are also investing in and concerned with the well-being of their employees have an excellent chance at success here.

Additional Resources

For more information about the realities of doing business in Asia, turn to the following resources: globaltalentunleashed. com/chapter-8

CHAPTER 9

Latin America, the Home of Relationship-Based Business

With a population of more than 650 million, Latin America (LATAM) is a very appealing global market.[22] It has long been recognized as an international hub for manufacturing operations thanks to its very competitive labor rates; Mexico's monthly minimum wage was US$156.90 in 2019, while Paraguay's was US$330, and Uruguay's was US$462.35. Nonetheless, it's worth noting that salaries in Latin America can be much more disparate than in other countries, so budget well above minimum wage if you hope to hire bilingual professionals in capital cities, especially with a degree or specialty. There is a lot of highly qualified talent to be sourced in LATAM—the time zone is ideal for collaboration with North America, and continuous improvements are being made to business infrastructure across the region.

Latin America is often seen as a homogenous region but actually spans North, Central, and South America and, in some opinions, the Caribbean. Entering the Latin American market is a business-savvy move, however, because, in contrast with Europe or Asia, most businesses can expand across the entire region using just three languages.

One downside of this region is ongoing security concerns; many organizations spend heavily on security personnel and technology to keep their premises and workforce safe. In addition, complying with complex local employment laws can be difficult and may be compounded when navigating in multiple languages. The labor laws are extremely complex. Because of the socialist history of the various countries in the region, employee protections are quite burdensome and expensive. This can be offset by the fact that it's often easy to find sufficient bilingual talent in LATAM, especially in technology roles.

However, these factors are just some of the considerations you'll want to weigh as you plan for a potential expansion into the LATAM region. Some of the most sought-after countries for regional offices are Brazil, Colombia, and Mexico. There's amazing talent in all of these locations. We also see quite a lot of tech talent being hired in Uruguay and Argentina.

Some of the requirements and issues to consider are culture, communication style, labor costs and negotiating, employment contracts, time off, termination, and infrastructure.

CULTURE

In many ways similar to Asian culture, Latin American culture is very family-centric and focused on relationship-building in business. In Mexico, the work environment varies by company. Some companies are very conservative in dress and behavior while others are informal and friendly. In the southern countries of South America, the work environment is more formal. Throughout the region, north or south, the highly qualified talent pool is vast and diverse.

Due to past and present governmental protectionist policies, employee protections can be very strong in some countries. While that may be great for employees, it can make hiring and firing workers much more complicated for employers.

Latin Americans place a great value on people and are very warm and welcoming in general. The value placed on relationships and relationship-building oftentimes is more important than keeping to a strict schedule. Arriving late to a meeting or event carries less of a negative impact that it might when doing business in America. Frequently, such tardiness occurs because the participants were focused on the people around them, rather than their watches. This is exacerbated by the fact that traffic in cities like São Paulo and Mexico City is nightmarish. It's almost expected that meetings will run long and people won't arrive on time to subsequent commitments.

Timeliness aside, should you arrive in Mexico or Brazil to business meetings, or elsewhere in LATAM, expect the red carpet to be rolled out. Your future colleagues and business partners will introduce you to the best of their culture, cities, families, and business. They'll take you out for a fabulous meal at a famous local restaurant and arrange the mariachis to come to your table. Set aside time to spend if they invite you to dinner or otherwise extend hospitality. Besides it being good for your business, you'll probably thoroughly enjoy the experience.

It's worth noting that there is a cultural and language divide between Brazil and the rest of the continent. Brazilians speak Portuguese while the rest of the region speaks Spanish. That's important to know because cultural stigmas and rivalry do exist between some countries that could impede cross-border business to some degree. If you hire a Chilean to cover the continent, don't assume that employee will speak Portuguese to cover Brazil, and vice versa; you'll need to either look to locals in each country or source trilingual talent. Luckily, this is perfectly doable.

There's some known rivalry between Argentina and Chile—not in a way that impedes business between the two, but local accents often facilitate relationships and, therefore, business deals. We do occasionally find bilingual people who are able to span the continent (digitally) coordinating matters for our customers, of course, but most people would advise you to hire for Brazil separately than the rest of South America. Central America and Mexico are also quite far, geographically, from South America, although we do see teams in Mexico covering all of LATAM. Finally, Miami may in some ways seem like the U.S. headquarters of LATAM, and many companies find talent there to supplement their operations in-region.

INCOMM PAYMENTS

InComm Payments has been operating within the global marketplace for nearly two decades. As barriers to global markets have been lowered and the propensity for e-commerce transactions has become commonplace, the company's business expansion has naturally accelerated as well. Its expansion and growth have been driven by industry/product growth, not new geographic penetration.

InComm became an international enterprise when it entered the Canadian market through an acquisition in 2002, followed by the UK and Japanese markets in 2006–2007.

Today, its strongest growth areas are in APAC (specifically Japan) and South America (Brazil).

After moving to a remote working model using Globalization Partners' global employment platform in several key locations, the company's operations continue to run smoothly, effectively supporting its employees' and clients' needs seamlessly. Globalization Partners provides all of the legal, HR, and finance infrastructure by hiring InComm team members through Globalization Partners' global subsidiaries in the locations where InComm doesn't have its own—so it doesn't have to set up its own in locations where it's only hiring a small headcount without other activity.

Although its preferred hiring approach has been location-centric to date, because the day-to-day work experience is different when you're "in the room," InComm has a number of team members who work from alternate locations. The business's leadership is very cognizant of the different employment experience for remote team members and has consistently strived to limit negative impacts.

COMMUNICATION STYLE

The focus on relationship-building carries over to communication style in this region. Communication is direct in some ways, almost assertive, but indirect in others, with a storytelling style shared for context. Those involved in conversations will want to be sure that everyone understands what is being requested and why, and what the background of the situation is. Providing the additional context ensures that everyone is informed and involved. Companies are very hierarchical, and it is expected that management will tell employees what to do. Indeed, businesses are almost patriarchal. The best businesses will be seen as taking care of their employees from a human perspective in a fatherly style. Employees who empower themselves to work for multinational companies are also ambitious and want the opportunity for growth. Providing a great atmosphere and the chance to grow professionally are the best ways to retain your team in LATAM.

Nearly all of LATAM speaks Spanish and a little English, but English-language skills aren't as predominant as a U.S. or Canadian employer would hope and are in high demand.

LABOR COSTS AND NEGOTIATING

Pay cycles and processes common in the U.S. are actually quite uncommon in LATAM, so you'll want to become familiar with the standard for the country in which you're operating.

Most countries in the region are fairly complicated from a labor law and union perspective. Due to the history of the region having a lot of communist and socialist influence, many laws are in place to protect the rights of workers. Other complications arise from currency matters and money laundering laws. Opening a bank account and wiring funds to and from Colombia, for example, requires our local lawyer to go to the bank and sign every time we send payroll from the U.S. This is because of the strict anti-money laundering regulations which stem from the region's history with the illegal drug trade. Tax laws in Brazil are also notoriously complicated, with up to 50 new tax laws being published each day.[23]

Throughout the region, most employees are paid monthly and, besides the normal monthly payouts, they're also entitled to a 13th-month bonus—and sometimes a 14th-month bonus. The 13th is a mandatory bonus payout, usually at Christmastime, often calculated as an average of the previous 12. This is important to be aware of as you're calculating the compensation package for a new hire—to an American, a US$5,000 monthly salary sounds like US$60,000 annually, but to someone expecting a 13th-month bonus, it sounds like an annual salary of US$65,000. In Argentina the 13th-month bonus must equal the highest monthly wages. And in Ecuador, Guatemala, Honduras, and Peru, workers also receive a 14th-month bonus at some point during the year. These 13th- and 14th-month bonus structures are important for your team members and part of the market norm. Even though it sounds unusual to HR departments that aren't expecting it, it's better to fit in with the local cultural norms related to payroll because it will deeply matter to your employees' sense of well-being.

Employees in some LATAM countries typically negotiate their salaries' "net," meaning they're negotiating for what they expect to land in their bank account after taxes are withheld. American employers almost always negotiate in gross terms, i.e., the pre-tax amount. Clarifying that you're offering a gross (pre-tax) offer to an employee is critical to avoid ending up back at the negotiating table later and disappointing your candidate when both parties realize that you've been comparing apples and oranges.

Social security and benefits costs add very high markup to salaries in some LATAM countries when figuring out the total cost of employment. There's a lot of fringe benefits offered to employees and a lot of taxes paid by the employer. Brazil is notoriously expensive in terms of the tax on top of the total cost of employment; employers are also subject to collective bargaining units (unions). Central and South America are nebulous regions in which to hire, but once you get past the various administrative hurdles, there's a huge market, great talent, and extraordinary future colleagues waiting on the other side.

VAYDA

Vayda is a high-tech regenerative farming startup aiming to bring regenerative farming systems to scale to help reverse climate change and grow better food. The company was operating globally from the start. Its founders and major investors are Canadian, partners and customers are in the U.S., and some company leaders and experienced talent are based in Brazil.

Going global was a necessity from the outset in order to connect the different aspects of the business, including capital, talent, and markets. Because of that international orientation, the company was founded as a remote operation and continues to build and grow as a distributed team.

That doesn't mean the sudden shift to a remote work model triggered by the pandemic was smooth across the board, however. Increased screen time sitting in front of a computer, the inability to read colleagues' signals or moods without in-person interactions, and the loss of casual ad hoc conversations that frequently result in sparks of creativity or unique insight were losses felt across the organization. But they were also balanced by the loss of a work commute, connecting with colleagues on a deeper level over the shared pandemic experience, an improved understanding of their home and work lives, and the new freedom to be able to hire the right talent, wherever that is, thanks to remote connectivity.

Since Vayda was built as a remote workforce, hiring team members in new global locations was just a regular part of doing business for the company. It continues to expand its team through Globalization Partners, which enables Vayda to hire anyone, anywhere, quickly and easily, without setting up branch offices in each country themselves.

Brazil

Some payment arrangements become complicated due to local labor law. In Brazil, for example, legislation dictates that, once hired by an employer, an employee's salary can only ever go up, not down. That can become problematic for sales professionals entitled to commission payments. In the U.S., those payments are made monthly on top of a salesperson's base salary. Moreover, in Brazil such payments increase the 13th-month salary and vacation payment, as these are calculated as an average of the commission, bonus, and salary earned during the year.

Thanks to strong labor unions in Brazil, employees receive legally mandated annual increases of around 2.5 percent to 3 percent every year, typically in May, to compensate for inflation. This is often in addition to the promotion cycle that your employees are likely to expect annually.

Brazil also has required benefits packages you'll want to review to ensure your organization is prepared to comply with those requirements. The total cost of employment in Brazil is often significantly higher than companies expect when factoring in all of the social insurance, taxes, and benefits that employers pay on top of the salary to employees.

When making a salary offer, make sure to specify that the figure is the monthly gross amount—not net. It is always best to be clear in discussions and paperwork. We highly recommend negotiating in gross terms because the net numbers may depend on employee circumstances and are hard to agree and stabilize. All employment documents, such as offer letters and compensation disclosures, are considered binding legal documents in Brazil, so only put in writing what you're willing to commit to.

Employees working as supervisors or managers with an exempt salary—meaning they are not paid overtime—are considered to be in a "position of trust." Such managerial positions should be paid approximately 40 percent more than their direct reports.

And the principle of comparable pay is also enforced in Brazil, whereby employees doing the same job in the same city are required to have the same title and pay.

Additional mandatory benefits include a meal voucher, transportation voucher, life insurance, and daycare assistance. Healthcare and dental care are not benefits that employers are responsible for, since health insurance is provided by the Brazilian government, but they are very common benefits. Some collective bargaining units negotiate insurance benefits over and above what's legally required by the government.

When employees are hired via Globalization Partners in Brazil to support our customers, all of the above benefits are handled as part of our existing infrastructure, and we manage the union so that the customer does not have to do so directly.

The focus on relationship-building carries over to communication style in this region. Communication is direct in some ways, almost assertive, but indirect in others, with a storytelling style shared for context. Those involved in

> *conversations want to be sure that everyone understands what is being requested and why, or what the background of the situation is.*

Mexico

Mexico has an incredible pool of highly talented and ambitious workers who are ready to make their mark on the world.

In Mexico City alone, there are more than 20 million people. About 13 percent of the population speaks English fluently. That's a talent pool of 2.6 million professionals that is highly targeted by large U.S. companies seeking to hire exceptional talent in the digital economy. The border cities of Monterrey and Tijuana are also hot spots for English-language talent acquisition for U.S. and Canadian companies.

The labor legislation in Mexico is not intuitive and may take some time to figure out.

In addition to the 13th-month salary, which is equivalent to 15 days' wages, due by December 20 each year, Mexican workers are also entitled to profit-sharing. Companies that have been in operation for at least one year must redistribute 10 percent of their pre-tax profits to employees.

The laws in Mexico are complicated and reflect the country's strong history with more socialist ideals. There is also VAT, corporate law, and other matters that are constantly evolving in Mexico.

We love Mexico as a place to hire great people and have engaged extraordinarily talented people there, not only for our own company but many of our customers.

ACTIVECAMPAIGN

ActiveCampaign is the leader in customer experience automation. Its mission is to help growing businesses make meaningful connections with their customers. Founded in 2003 in Chicago with a sole employee, the company as of May 2021 has more than 150,000 customers in 170 countries and more than 850 employees throughout the world, including hubs in Chicago, Indianapolis, Dublin, and Sydney.

ActiveCampaign has been a global company since its first customer in Mexico. As of 2020, more than half of its 130,000 customers are based outside of the U.S. Being location-agnostic from the get-go is a significant reason for the company's rapid growth. More than 40,000 customers and 300 employees were onboarded in 2020 alone, and the pace of growth is only accelerating. The business intends to reach over 1,000 employees in 2021.

The company is unusual in that it had over 50 percent of its business come from outside of the U.S. prior to any hiring in other regions. This speaks to ActiveCampaign's unique international approach, which has fueled its momentum. The company opened its first international office in Sydney in 2018. By opening that office with customer support, customer success, and sales team members, they were able to better serve their customers in the APAC region. This allowed them to support customers any time of day. Since then, ActiveCampaign has opened offices in Dublin and, thanks to a partnership with Globalization Partners, has a significant presence in Brazil to better support customers in those regions.

Their teams around the world each play an integral part in their momentum on a daily basis. The customer support teams are engaging with local customers and sharing feedback with the product development teams to make the platform even stronger. One example of where they have proved their localization efforts is Brazil, where ActiveCampaign launched its first localized currency and language. Efforts like these are helping the sales teams introduce ActiveCampaign to new businesses and keep the company growing.

Having everyone working remotely was a significant cultural shift for the team, which was part of a strong in-office culture pre-pandemic. Now that all employees are working entirely remotely, the company has swapped its in-person perks for benefits like a quarterly work-from-home stipend and virtual classes that cover everything from yoga to professional development. The team also introduced mental health resources like free access to therapy for all employees, along with subscriptions to meditation and coaching apps like Calm, Soothe, and Modern Health. Employee resource groups were also formed for employees who are isolating alone as well as for employees who are parents. The company's managers are listening to their employees' needs and constantly introducing benefits accordingly.

ActiveCampaign plans to hire aggressively around each of its hubs and will continue to expand its international focus and hubs over time using Globalization Partners' global employment platform. The future for the business is all about being flexible.

EMPLOYMENT CONTRACTS

The process of hiring employees varies by country in LATAM, so it's important to check on local customs and requirements. In Argentina, for example, strong labor unions provide exceptional protections for employees. That means that employers are often at a disadvantage in negotiations. In Chile, workers like a local connection to a potential employer, so bringing on board local residents first can help greatly there.

Employees often ask to be paid in U.S. dollars, which fluctuate less than some local currencies. There are a few countries in LATAM where this is legally acceptable, but be mindful to check the details before agreeing to pay an international employee in U.S. dollars.

Brazil

Given that documents related to hiring are considered contractual, you'll want to be very careful what you put in writing related to a new hire offer and agreement. Your offer letter and employment contract should be presented in Portuguese and indicated in the local currency, Brazilian Real (BRL). The contract should also include details regarding benefits and termination policies.

There is a probationary period permitted in Brazil of up to 90 days, and a contract can be terminated at the end of that 90 days with final pay also including unused vacation and a prorated 13th-month payout.

Employee-friendly countries tend to have courts that rule in favor of the employee, and much of the litigation in some countries has to do with overtime compensation.

Employees in Brazil are union members and are entitled to annual increases as negotiated by the union. Once the increase is agreed upon, it is often backdated to August 1 of the prior year, depending on the relevant union's norm. Employees who have changed employers since that time are entitled to prorated payment of that increase.

Mexico

Employment contracts are mandatory in Mexico, and there is no option for at-will employment. However, there are differing lengths of agreements: indefinite and definite. Indefinite contracts have no set end date, and most professional contracts are indefinite.

Contracts are important here because there is no unemployment insurance, and employees want a level of security regarding their job. There is a probationary period, however, so employees who are not a good fit can be let go without major inconvenience to the employer within that period.

TIME OFF

Public holidays are mandatory paid days off. In Brazil, there are typically 12 paid holidays each year. Mexico has seven national holidays, plus election day every six years.

Brazil

Many LATAM countries have laws regarding maximum work hours. In Brazil, the workweek can be as long as 44 hours, made up of five eight-hour workdays with an hour for lunch, plus a four-hour workday on Saturday. Some companies elect to have slightly longer workdays during the week and then take Saturdays off, but the law prohibits having employees work more than 44 hours total in a week without additional compensation.

After 12 months of employment, professional workers in Brazil are entitled to 30 days of vacation, which is typically divided either into 1) a 20-day holiday and a 10-day break, 2) three periods with one being a minimum of 14 days and two a minimum of 5 days each, or 3) a solid 30 days off in a row.

Employees are also paid one-third of a month's salary as a holiday bonus.

Sick days are paid up to 15 days with a doctor's note. More than 15 days are covered by the National Institute of Social Security rather than the employer at a fixed rate. Benefits must continue to be paid, however.

New mothers are entitled to 120 days of maternity leave and cannot be let go due to pregnancy. New fathers are entitled to five days of paid paternity leave as long as it is requested in advance.

Mexico

In Mexico, employees are mandated at least one day of rest per week. If they work more than 48 hours, they are entitled to overtime, though there is also a cap on the number of overtime hours that can be worked in a week.

Mexican workers are also entitled to vacation days. After one year of employment, they are entitled to six days of vacation, which increases the longer they are with the company. After eight years, they are entitled to 14 vacation days.

TERMINATION

Although it is certainly possible to terminate an employee in LATAM, it is much more involved than in other parts of the world, due to the employee protections encoded into law.

Brazil

In Brazil, either employer or employee may terminate an employment contract with 30 days' notice; payment for that period can also be made by the employer in lieu of 30 days of work. Every year that employees work, they are entitled to three more days of notice, up to a total of 60 additional days, for a total of 90 days' notice required. When employees leave, they must be paid:

- Pay owed up to their last day

- Unused and accrued vacation pay plus a third of this total as a bonus

- Prorated 13th-month bonus

- Any remaining bonuses, overtime, or benefits prorated to the date of termination

Each month, employers must pay the equivalent of eight percent of employees' salary into an unemployment account. When they are let go, they receive what's in the account plus an additional 40 percent from their former employer as long as they were terminated without cause. If they are terminated with cause or resign, the 40 percent supplemental payment is not required. However, proving cause is often challenging, and most employers forgo trying to do so in most cases.

Brazil offers 12 reasons employers can terminate with cause, but doing so often leads to lawsuits by former employees. For that reason, many employers prefer to negotiate and mutually agree on a separation package, which might halve the costs for the employer.

Infrastructure

The infrastructure in Central and South America is continuously improving, and a large percentage of workers go into an office to work. The Economic Commission for Latin America and the Caribbean reports that 67 percent of the region's population has internet access. We have found that work from home *works* in LATAM, but there historically has been a strong cultural preference to go to the office in many locations, due to the highly social nature of people in the workplace. Whether this changes permanently due to the pandemic is yet to be seen. One-off tech workers who agree to work from home will undoubtedly be well equipped to do so, but more junior employees may need help ensuring a strong Wi-Fi connection and comfortable at-home workspace.

Additional Resources

For more information about the realities of doing business in Latin America, turn to the following resources: globaltalentunleashed.com/chapter-9

CHAPTER 10

The Middle East's Glittering Cities and Business Opportunities

The Middle East is one of the most fascinating places in the world to travel and do business. Within the Middle East, the United Arab Emirates (UAE) is by far the most popular location international companies choose when setting up a local entity. Having sprung out of the desert in the 1970s after the discovery of oil, entire glittering cities and societies have been built by people whose great-grandparents were nomads in the desert, living in ancient tribal traditions. The culture is strong and vibrant, and the Emirati people and government are working hard to lessen their dependency on oil and create a nation-state with an economy that will last long into the future.

As a nation of approximately one million people, the Emiratis had to import talent in order to create the extraordinary success they've had in the last several decades. They did so by creating one of the most unique economies in one of the safest countries in the world. Almost 90 percent of the people living and working in the Emirates are expatriates, or citizens of other countries, and the economy is run almost entirely by expatriates at all levels of society.[24]

From a labor perspective, the Middle East is its own situation and entirely unlike the rest of the world.

The United Arab Emirates comprises seven Emirates: Abu Dhabi, Ajman, Dubai, Fujairah, Ras Al Khaimah, Sharjah, and Umm Al Quwain. Most businesses land in Dubai unless their local teams need to facilitate government relations, in which case they're more likely to hire in Abu Dhabi.

While the UAE is very business friendly, it is also regulation-heavy and rather complex to navigate initially, simply because it takes some time to understand its unique structure. One of the first decisions to be made involves where to physically locate the business or your employees. There are two options: 1) on the mainland or 2) in one of approximately 45 free zones. The free zones are areas where 100 percent foreign ownership is allowed, as well as free inflow and outflow of capital. This is not the same as "offshore," so, in order to understand this fully, consult a local lawyer who can help. A professional can guide you to ascertain what's more appropriate for you and whether using an EOR is an option.

CULTURE

Unlike many other places, hiring in the UAE is unusual because nearly all employees in the region are expatriates. That means that a visa will be required for non-UAE citizens to be able to work in the country—a visa your company will need to sponsor, unless the employee is engaged on your behalf via an EOR that can sponsor the visa.

One quirk of the UAE business requirements is that they are tied to office space and visa validity. The size of a company's leased office space determines how many visas or employees the company is permitted to sponsor. Due to the office-space-to-worker ratio requirement, office space in premium areas is expensive. This is how the Emirate has funded much of its building infrastructure.

Business dress is on the formal side except on Thursdays, the last day of the workweek, when dress becomes a little less formal—though still business appropriate.

Expatriates are legally permitted to drink in designated situations, but it's highly regulated. Weekend brunch (where only expats are allowed to drink) is the social highlight of the week for non-Emiratis.

Emiratis are at the top of the social hierarchy in the UAE, and expatriates are expected to defer to them. The UAE is a highly socially stratified society. However, many equal opportunity campaigns are emerging, such as laws for equal pay, and women are now represented at the highest government levels. In general, when hiring sales executives, our customers prefer to hire Arab-speaking men because those men will be able to socialize with the high-ranking Emiratis in business and government. Caucasian men are the next best choice and are also often able to navigate society well. Everyone else fills the other roles, ranging from engineers to office workers and everything in between. Professional women are able to be successful in the Emiratis, but business relationships may be affected by the gender division in after-hours networking, which very much matters for success. It is considered very safe for professional women to travel solo in the UAE.

The UAE is a place where local norms must be rigorously respected. Acceptable social behavior is clearly stipulated and enforced, adding to the security in the country. Be extremely respectful of the local culture when traveling anywhere in the Middle East. Women and men can wear business pantsuits, and women should wear a shirt beneath that covers the entire chest up to the neckline.

Dubai is permissive regarding clothing, but it's always considerate to mind the local culture, especially if you're there on business. Wear loose, professional clothing to be respectful and considerate. Is it legal to wear a short skirt and high heels? Yes, but it's not very discreet, and it's inappropriate—kind of like someone wearing a string bikini to a mall in New York.

COMMUNICATION STYLE

Business relationships in the UAE are built on trust and familiarity, which starts with small talk and casual conversation before talking business. It's customary for businesspeople to compliment others with whom they are dealing, and it's expected that you will return compliments as a way of articulating your appreciation of your partners. Praise your host and others around you to show respect.

It is also important and wise to bring a gift to your hosts. Chocolates, dates, or nuts are nice options; make sure the wrapping is aesthetically pleasing and elegant. Something nice from your hometown is also a good option. If you're meeting with Emiratis, expect time for coffee, snacks, and conversation about social interests as well as time spent discussing business. The Emiratis are excellent hosts and will extend warmth to you, if they've invited you into their business circle. They will want to get to know you and are likely to extend every courtesy to you. If you're meeting with other expats, Western business culture norms more or less apply.

Cost Structure and Terms of Offers

The UAE is not an inexpensive place to do business, but the cost structure is significantly different from most places. The country doesn't collect income taxes, but it does charge hefty business licensing fees and requires companies to sponsor office space for every employee visa it sponsors.

Most compensation packages in the UAE are paid as a salary plus various allowances for expatriate-related costs and commissions as appropriate for the job. We recommend negotiating a gross "total compensation" that includes all allowances rather than negotiating housing, transportation, and education allowances on top of a base salary. When the negotiation is complete and it's time to put everything into the contract, the total amount will be broken out into the various allowances typically offered to expatriates and as required for employment contracts by your local advisors.

Besides normal compensation, companies also need to factor in the mandatory end-of-service gratuity if they hire expats, which is the equivalent of 21 days of pay for each of the first five years and 30 days of pay for each year after that, with a maximum gratuity of two years' salary. Employers are also responsible for covering the cost of flying expats back to their home countries or wherever they were working prior to arriving in the UAE. By law, an employee has to be flown out of the country as quickly as within 10 days after their job ends in some jurisdictions because residency permits are contingent upon work permits sponsored by the employer. This can cause considerable stress for employees upon termination, and is very important to keep in mind.

In practice, longer termination notice periods are often informally arranged to give the employee time to find a solution, such as a new employer or work permit sponsor. It's especially important for employers to handle terminations with grace and respect, because here, even more than other locations, people's lives are dependent on their employment.

Case in point: We once had a Syrian national whose California-based customer wanted to terminate his work in Qatar, which has employment laws similar to the UAE for expatriates. This happened during the peak of the Syrian Civil War. We explained to the end customer that if they wanted to terminate the individual's work abruptly and he was unable to find a new employer immediately, he faced having to depart Qatar with his family and go home to a war zone.

With this explanation and a few solutions in hand, we were able to problem-solve with both the employee and the end customer so that the employee could stay in-country. We would have never put an employee in that situation. In many cases, your employees in the Middle East will have purchased homes, have children enrolled in school, and otherwise have built lives in their adopted country. Their entire lives depend on their employer and their work permit eligibility, and so a sudden job loss can be catastrophic. Thankfully, we have always been able to find solutions for employees in these situations. Our customers also have been understanding and gracious of the time it can take to conduct a human-centered solution that works for everyone. The typical win-win solution is usually a short period of advance notice that the end is in sight. This gives the employee time to find a new job and transfer his or her work permit.

Business relationships in the UAE are built on trust and familiarity, which starts with small talk and casual conversation before talking business. It's customary for businesspeople to

> *compliment others with whom they are dealing, and it's expected that you will return compliments as a way of articulating your appreciation of your partners.*

EMPLOYMENT CONTRACTS

There are two kinds of employment contracts in the UAE at present:

- Limited, fixed-term

- Unlimited

The difference is that a limited-term contract can last for up to two years but can be renewed. Limited contracts also require notice of termination of one to three months by either party that they are terminating the contract. An end-of-service gratuity is then paid on the conclusion of the contract.

An unlimited contract is the most common type of arrangement and has no specific term. Employer or employee can terminate the employment agreement with 30 days' notice and justification.

To hire an employee in the UAE, an official job offer must be made in writing, which then becomes the basis of an employment contract. Once signed, employers can then obtain from the UAE Ministry of Labor: 1) a work permit, also known as an establishment labor card, and 2) an establishment immigration card. Obtaining these cards can be done online and is fairly simple if you gather all the required documentation, but they can take a while to process.

All compensation amounts must be stated in the local currency, which is the United Arab Emirates Dirham (AED), not in U.S. dollars (USD).

Contracts are fairly straightforward, but it is important to ensure that employees read and understand all the terms laid out in an offer letter and subsequent work contract. It is the *employer's* responsibility to explain each provision and confirm that the employee understands what it means. This law was put into place to protect low-wage earners who are often brought in from other countries and may not understand the nuances of what they're signing, but it is applicable to all employees, including the white-collar professionals our customers typically engage.

Once a contract is signed, it is deemed officially accepted and can't be changed by either party without mutual agreement. The contract is submitted as part of the visa application process and goes into the government record. The UAE authorities also check the amounts paid to the employees each month against the contract, via the Wage Protection System (WPS), to ensure that the employees are indeed being paid the amount agreed. This is done to ensure that employees are not being held hostage to unfair terms such as employers not paying the amounts agreed before the employee came into the country, which would essentially leave the employees trapped and dependent on the employer without a means of terminating their employment. The UAE authorities put that safety check in place for the protection of its expatriate workforce.

All expatriates must receive a medical exam before a work permit will be issued, limited to a torso X-ray and blood tests. The employee has 14 days to submit the results of the medical exam to the Ministry of Labor (MOL) to qualify for the work permit and receive a copy of his or her fully executed employment agreement.

Once the MOL approves an employee's work permit, the visa application can then continue. First, however, the MOL will check to see if there is a citizen of the UAE who is qualified to fill the position and that the company is registered as an employer there. If no issues arise, the application will be approved and employees can receive their visa at the airport upon their arrival, or the application for transferring a visa from one employer to another will be approved.

RL CANNING INC.

Chicago-based RL Canning Inc. is an information technology services provider with approximately 400 employees. The company's global expansion began with launching its services offering into Europe, establishing entities in the UK, France, and Spain. Today it operates in 46 states and 19 countries. RL Canning's expansion leveraged Globalization Partners' global employment platform to support payroll, benefits, legal compliance, and human resources, allowing it to meet the complex demands of its core business. RL Canning was also able to ensure compliance while scaling quickly. By using Globalization Partners' global employment platform, it didn't have to set up its own entity.

TIME OFF

Interestingly, the workweek in the UAE is from Sunday to Thursday, with Friday and Saturday reserved as the weekend. That requires a little planning or coordinating with teams in the West, who are on a Monday through Friday work schedule.

Fridays are mandated days off. If employees are required to work on Friday, they might then be entitled to another full day off, plus the equivalent of overtime for that Friday work of up to 50 percent of their daily pay. This is mostly true for low-skill workers. Saturday is the second day of the weekend, but it's considered reasonable to have employees work a half day on Saturday if the normal workweek is insufficient for business purposes.

Employees are limited by law to a maximum eight-hour workday and no more than 48 hours in a week. Some fields, such as food service, hospitality, and security, allow a maximum nine-hour workday. Public employees typically work a five and a half or six-hour workday, from 7:30 a.m. to 2:30 p.m. Private companies make their own hours, and the schedule follows similar hours to Western businesses, but on a Sunday through Thursday schedule rather than Monday through Friday.

Although new employees with less than six months of service are not entitled to vacation days, other employees are. Those with between six and 12 months of employment are entitled to two days of vacation per month employed. After one year of employment, the employee automatically gets 30 days of vacation per year, which is the standard in the UAE. Any unused vacation days may be accrued and used later or paid out. Your employees will typically fly to their home country and spend it with their families. This vacation time is most often taken in August. Most employers pay for the round-trip flight, and it is often negotiated in the employment contract whether the employer will also pay for family members' flights, whether there's a cap on the amount spent, and other details. This time is valued and important to your employees. If they take the time in August, it's convenient for everyone, because many people in-country are also taking vacation at that time, and it can be a business dead zone.

Similarly, with sick leave, after three months of continuous service following a probationary period of up to six months (meaning, probationary period plus three months), employees are entitled to up to 90 days of sick leave per year, paid depending on length of illness. If there is no probationary period, the employee is eligible for sick leave after three months of continuous service. The first 15 days are paid at full wage. Between 16 and 45 days, half wages are paid, and over 45 days, there is no pay given. While this is the minimum requirement according to federal law, most Western firms pay the full salary. However, if employees' illness or injury is the direct result of misconduct, they are not entitled to any pay for their days off.

Women with at least one year of employment are entitled to 45 paid days of maternity leave and can request 10 more without pay. Men are entitled to five days of paternity leave during the first six months following the child's birth.

Muslim employees are permitted a one-time unpaid leave of up to 30 days to participate in the Hajj, an annual pilgrimage to Mecca, Saudi Arabia, which they are expected to do at least once in their lifetime. Should an employee request this, it is a cause to be celebrated and honored, as it is considered an extraordinarily meaningful and life-changing trip.

Besides the vacation time, there are approximately 12 official holidays per year that employees are entitled to with pay.

TERMINATION

Depending on whether the employment contract was limited or unlimited, termination may only require 30 days' notice and justification, as with an unlimited contract, or it may become a negotiation if the employer wants to sever the relationship before the end of the two-year term (or whatever the stipulated length). One reason most of our customers don't choose a fixed-term contract is that if the employer-employee relationship doesn't go well, it's more likely that the employer will be asked to pay the entire term of the contract, even if the employee is no longer working.

At the end of a limited contract, as has already been mentioned, the employer must pay an end-of-service gratuity and repatriation costs.

INFRASTRUCTURE

The infrastructure in the UAE is among the most advanced in the world, with state-of-the-art technology, telecommunications capabilities, and transportation, supported by continued investment in the region's ability to participate in the world economy. There are no issues with connectivity or transportation that will limit your team's ability to work.

ADDITIONAL RESOURCES

For more information about the realities of doing business in the UAE, turn to the following resources: globaltalentunleashed. com/chapter-10

CHAPTER 11

Canada

The most prominent destination we see American companies expand into first is Canada. While culturally the U.S. and Canada are very similar, there are some differences regarding employment that you'll want to be aware of before finalizing plans to engage a team across the border.

Provincial rules and regulations vary widely, so it matters a lot whom you're engaging, where they live, and why you're choosing to engage a team in Canada. For example, Toronto is one of the most popular cities for global offices. Montreal, to the east, is in the French-speaking province of Quebec and is much different from the rest of the country culturally and legally—it's much more like France. Canada has federal laws, but much like the U.S., each province has regulations you'll want to pay particular attention to.

CULTURE

Perhaps to an even greater degree than in the U.S., Canadians treat others as equals. Professional input is generally requested from everyone, unlike in hierarchical cultures where status determines the right to speak or provide feedback. Canada is very inclusive.

Where Americans are known for their willingness to work long hours, Canadians are similar, but not quite to the same extreme. Canadians are more likely to take breaks during the day and are not as dedicated to working consistently long hours. Canada has a slightly more moderate approach to work.

COMMUNICATION STYLE

Whereas Americans have a very direct communication style that leaves little room for misinterpretation, Canadians are a little softer in how they approach conversations. They are more likely to provide some context for their request or response, rather than jumping in to assert their preferences.

Perhaps due to the French influence, Canadians are also more likely to engage in some small talk, leading into emails or meetings. They may chit-chat for a couple of minutes before getting down to business, like their European counterparts, and generally focus more on relationships between business partners.

Setting up and managing a legal entity in Canada is more complicated than one might expect, primarily due to the web of tax regulations that come into play between the U.S. and Canada and between Canadian federal law and provincial law. Should you prefer to go the traditional entity setup route, getting a lawyer experienced in U.S./Canadian tax law to advise on the appropriate corporate structure is strongly recommended. In addition, managing GST (goods and services tax) may be necessary for your Canadian entity as well as your U.S. business. Incorporating and hiring people directly in Canada requires strong local support and is not as straightforward as one would expect. Most complications can be minimized by working via a competent Employer of Record. Even so, it's always recommended to check with your advisors on anything related to structuring and tax, including whether an Employer of Record is a good fit for your business.

VYOPTA

Collaboration intelligence company Vyopta is a global leader in comprehensive monitoring and analytics for collaboration performance management and workspace insights. By integrating insights from multi-vendor unified communications (UC) and collaboration vendors and IoT devices, Austin-based Vyopta helps organizations deliver the best UC user experience and optimize their UC and real estate investments.

Vyopta helps hundreds of organizations worldwide, including managed service providers, in dozens of industries.

International companies wanting to use Vyopta gave the company the opportunity to expand its team outside the U.S., venturing into Canada first. By 2018, when team members were needed in the UK and India, Vyopta turned to Globalization Partners to add support in different time zones. Globalization Partners made hiring a global remote team almost seamlessly easy by eliminating the complex legal, tax, and HR issues traditionally associated with international hires.

Having made a commitment from the start to only hire the best, from anywhere, remote work has been part of the Vyopta DNA for many years. Because more than 80 percent of the Vyopta team was already working remote pre-Covid, moving the entire team to remote work was seamless.

While switching to 100 percent remote work was easy, keeping everyone mentally engaged and morale high has been challenging. Mental health issues are something that every company is dealing with and will have to deal with for years to come. Vyopta has become much more aware of and sensitive to this new reality.

Not having to spend many hours en route to and from work has been a positive for Vyopta team members who now work remotely. The main downside reported has been getting used to sharing space with other adults and children also working from home; everyone is home 24/7. Quiet space—any space—for calls is limited for some. Needing to watch over young ones and elderly family members during "work" hours can also be difficult, so there have been conference calls with children and pets in attendance.

One of the biggest advantages of expanding globally has been enabling Vyopta to better support customers 24/7. Round-the-clock coverage helps ensure they are achieving the maximum value possible in using the Vyopta solution. The company's business in Europe and Australia now makes up 20 percent of its total annual revenue.

Cost Structure

Pay in Canada is generally aligned with pay in the U.S., or very similar. One important difference is that employees below managerial positions are eligible for overtime, but this varies by province. Tracking time, even among professionals, is a best practice from a legal perspective, although from an HR perspective, most senior professionals refuse to do it. One way some companies balance this legal best practice with the HR reality is to have employees who choose not to track their time by the hour, sign an agreement that they'll notify their employer if they're working overtime. This way, it's clear that the employer agreed to paying any overtime that was worked and that the burden is on the employee to let the company know if more compensation is owed.

EMPLOYMENT CONTRACTS

Canadian employees are protected by comprehensive federal and provincial labor laws. Some U.S. companies try to avoid the complexity of hiring Canadians according to the legal requirements and hire them as independent contractors as a workaround. However, because Canada has a very limited definition of independent contractor, it's likely that those contractors would be categorized as employees by the government. Besides potentially incurring fines and penalties for the misclassification, a U.S. company directly employing people in Canada opens its U.S. company to corporate taxes in Canada. Finally, without a proper employment contract, your company's IP ownership, non-compete, and confidentiality requirements might not be adequately protected. Thus, it's much better to hire employees from the start if that is what you know you need and get the proper terms in place to protect your business.

As in other countries, it is possible to negotiate a fixed-term contract, although many Canadian courts will assume such a contract was converted to unlimited after several extensions, or if the employee continued to work after the contract term ended. Most companies hire employees on indefinite contracts.

A written employment contract is strongly recommended so that there is a record of what the two parties agreed to at the start of the employment relationship. Except in the province of Quebec, where contracts must be in French or both French and English, contracts are written in English. As part of the contract, the salary offer (stated in Canadian dollars), benefits, and termination notice periods should be outlined.

Each province has standards regarding restrictions on work hours; many have limitations on the maximum hours employees are permitted to work in a week. However, once an employee has exceeded the maximum, overtime pay of one and a half times their standard pay is required. In Quebec, overtime starts after 40 hours, while in Ontario the cutoff is 44 hours a week.

Employees in Canada have access to free public healthcare, which is managed by each province, but professionals expect employers to offer private healthcare that is over and above the free care. The cost of the supplemental care, which typically includes life insurance, disability, medical, dental, and vision, is significantly less than what employers are used to paying in the U.S.

Each province is subject to the federal contribution rates for the Canadian social security system, which covers Employment Insurance programs and the Canada Pension Plan. The exception is Quebec, which sets contribution rates to Employment Insurance, as well as its own Quebec Pension Plan and Quebec Parental Insurance Plan. All employees have a percentage of their pay deducted each month and contributed into the system up to an annual maximum contribution. It is the employer's responsibility to determine the correct amount to be deducted on the employees' behalf.

Employers must also withhold income tax from employee paychecks.

INFORCE TECHNOLOGIES

Inforce Technologies is a boutique technology implementation, integration, and consulting group focused exclusively on the insurance domain. The firm is headquartered in Cleveland with resource locations in Toronto and Kraljevo, Serbia. Its 82 team members consist primarily of software engineers, quality assurance analysts, and project managers.

The firm's growth is due, in large part, to its hiring success in Serbia. In 2019, Inforce Technologies opened an office in Kraljevo led by two Serbian employees who had returned to the area after working in the U.S. for more than 10 years. They moved back to Kraljevo in order to care for aging parents. Instead of separating them from the company, Inforce Technologies offered them the opportunity to work remotely. Although this was the first time in the company's history remote work had been offered, this flexibility opened up an entire untapped pool of exceedingly competent and talented team members. Today, that office has nearly 60 team members.

As a technology company, the actual switch to remote work during the pandemic was relatively seamless. Team members had already been given the flexibility to work from home two days per week, and employees were also permitted to work anywhere in the world for up to two weeks at a time, so the necessary internal infrastructure was already in place for employees to work from out of the office. That made global expansion easier than for most companies.

However, there are a number of employees that prefer to work regularly in the office. The office is their sanctuary from home. This is especially true for team members with children and those employees who do not have a home office setup that is as comfortable or equipped as the office.

Inforce Technologies has had much success expanding into Southeastern Europe, providing comparatively lucrative compensation packages for the region, while still being able to offer resources at a reduced rate from what U.S.-based team members would cost. These team members also work during U.S. business hours, which provides a significant competitive advantage.

Workers in Southeastern Europe have a very strong work ethic, technical aptitude, and a culture that is similar to the U.S. What is especially fulfilling is seeing team members earn lucrative career opportunities unavailable anywhere else in the region.

By comparison, resources in Canada, where Inforce Technologies also has a presence, can be costly. Compensation packages cater more to U.S. employees, yet there are additional costs associated with these team members because the firm does not yet have a legal entity presence in the region and instead leverages Globalization Partners as the legal Employer of Record. Globalization Partners handles the company's legal, administrative, and HR issues, which frees it from having to navigate those in-house and saves the company considerable time and expenses it would otherwise incur.

Although almost all Inforce Technologies employees are currently working remotely, the firm is rethinking its physical office presence, starting with the U.S. For team members in Serbia who prefer to work in the office, the company is exploring staggered office workdays there.

As Inforce Technologies continues to grow and its comfort level continues to increase with hiring remotely, the firm remains committed to delivering excellent onboarding, training, and ongoing support with a strong company culture. That is its challenge. Consequently, the company is continually looking at ways to bring the team together to keep them connected and positive.

TIME OFF

Employees are entitled to time off for paid vacation days, the number of which varies by province. Two weeks of vacation after one year of employment is fairly standard. For professional-level positions, three to four weeks is more typical, plus federal and provincial holidays.

Earned vacation must be permitted to be accrued or banked for later use; vacation time does not expire at the end of the year.

Vacation pay is determined based on an employee's salary and multiplying it by 4 percent for those with two weeks of vacation and 6 percent for those entitled to three weeks off.

Most provinces do not have a requirement for a specific number of paid sick days per year. However, the country's Employment Insurance does provide long-term sick leave, if needed.

Unpaid maternity leave averages about 17 weeks but can be extended as long as 63 weeks when combined with parental leave, depending on eligibility and province. Unlike the rest of Canada, Quebec also offers paternity leave exclusively for fathers. The government also offers employment insurance benefits during leave, if parents apply and are approved.

There are also a number of public holidays each year, from national holidays like New Year's Day, Canada Day, and Labour Day to provincial-specific holidays, such as Islander Day in Prince Edward Island, National Holiday in Quebec, and Heritage Day in Nova Scotia, to name a few.

Pay in Canada is generally aligned with pay in the U.S., or is very similar, but some employees are eligible for overtime. Tracking time, even among professionals, is best practice from a legal perspective to protect the company. However, few

senior professionals want to do it—so an HR middle ground
solution is often advised.

TERMINATION

Most Canadian employment contracts have a 90-day probationary period, though they can vary slightly by province. However, even if employees are terminated during their first three months, they may be entitled to a severance package.

Since at-will employment does not exist in Canada, companies operating there are required to either provide statutory notice regarding the termination of their employment or payment in lieu of notice. Typical statutory notice is one week for service under one year, which increases with the number of years of service. Reasonable notice, on the other hand, is somewhat subjective and is based on an employee's length of service, position in the company, age, and ability to find employment elsewhere. There are required minimum payments that employers cannot negotiate away, but these amounts are fairly reasonable.

Severance pay in Canada is based on a multiplier of weekly wages and years and months of service, with a maximum amount of 26 weeks of pay.

ADDITIONAL RESOURCES

For more information about the realities of doing business in Canada, turn to the following resources: globaltalentunleashed. com/chapter-11

Chapter 12

Employee Engagement

The process you use to recruit, hire, and onboard employees, whether U.S.-based or global, has a long-lasting impact on employee engagement and retention. How employees feel when they first join your organization and how you treat them shapes their attitude, work ethic, and loyalty to the company. As renowned poet Maya Angelou said, "People will forget what you said; people will forget what you did; but people will never forget how you made them feel." That's a great inspirational line for any HR team because, ultimately, everything about the way you treat your team affects your ability to be successful.

Once you have great talent in place, it's expensive when they leave. It's much more cost-effective, productive, and efficient to do your best to hold onto the employees you've brought on board. You've already looked into their background, interviewed them, and decided they would be an asset to your business, so after investing all that time and energy, doesn't it make sense to try and give them the best chance to be successful in their new role?

In general, we've found that our customers are pleasantly surprised and delighted with the international talent they're able to bring on board. Sometimes it can be a little intimidating for executives to hire talent in places they've only seen on maps or in movies, but once they start hiring, barriers dissipate and they roll out the welcome mat—because great talent anywhere is a tremendous asset.

CREATING A WELCOMING EMPLOYEE EXPERIENCE

To that end, the employee experience, from the start of the hiring process, will determine how engaged and invested your employees become. At a minimum, new employees need to feel that you care about them, that you care about the experience they'll have working for your company, and that you're investing in their training and professional development. Conversely, companies that hire new employees without training them, introducing them to their colleagues, or making them feel that they're part of a team and yet expect them to be successful from day one, are frequently disappointed.

If your employee onboarding process is careless and haphazard and you have a new employee in Singapore (where there is a 12-hour time difference), he or she might be in a situation where no one in the home office makes an effort to connect with them regularly. That's a problem, and it will generally result in employees leaving to work for a company that makes them feel like they're a team member, not a lone wolf with little chance of becoming successful. When that inevitably happens, you're back at square one, beginning a search to replace that lone wolf. It can become a vicious, expensive, and unproductive cycle unless you stop to look at what you're doing to engage and retain your people. While this seems like common sense, we have found that some companies would be well-advised to put themselves in their employees' shoes for a day, especially when hiring internationally. Doing so would make their businesses much more successful.

If you look at your profit and loss statement, it's likely you'll see a vast majority of your costs are spent on payroll. Most modern businesses are universal in that regard. Finding and onboarding talent is extremely challenging and expensive, but even more so when done poorly. You can have a fantastic return on your investment in talent, but it requires more than dollars. You also have to take the care and attention required to onboard, train, and retain your best talent for the long haul and inspire them to give you their best.

Every time a long-term employee walks out the door, you're losing a significant source of institutional knowledge and business history—knowledge that will be difficult to replace.

Looking back over Globalization Partners' business history, we've doubled our workforce every year for the last several years—and are accelerating even faster in 2021. We went from 87 internal employees in 2018 to 187 at the end of 2019 and 320 at the end of 2020, and we will have almost 1,000 employees at the end of 2021. Filling 600 seats in one year is a vast endeavor, but imagine if, in addition to filling those 600 new roles, we also had to find replacements for people who were leaving as quickly as we could fill seats. Then it would become nearly impossible to reach our growth goal. There are just too many moving parts for a company to be productive when you have a revolving door—when an even larger percentage of your costs are attributed to human resources, it's like treading water. Setting up employees to fail from the start is unfair, a terrible business strategy, and creates negativity around your company that everyone who encounters it perceives. Making an investment in retaining your people is much more productive and profitable, on top of being the right thing to do. It's win-win for all involved.

4 Key Factors to

Hiring a Talented Global Team

A fast-growing company needs more than just a bigger team – here's how to hire the right team when your company begins going global.

1 Fit Your Company Values

While you can't copy and paste your home office's culture into a new country, it's crucial to define your core values and choose candidates that fit.

Then, let offices located in different regions of the world develop a unique culture, while aligning with headquarters on what matters.

2 Find Employees That Can Wear Multiple Hats

As your company expands globally, it's important to bring on team members able to fill multiple evolving roles, meeting the needs of your company as you grow quickly in a specific country or region.

3 Prioritize Diversity

Companies in the top quartiles for gender and racial diversity are 15% and 35% more likely to have higher-than-average industry returns, respectively.

And 90% of global employees describe their companies as diverse – which shows that diversity is crucial to company culture in a global environment.

Focus on a candidate pool of varied abilities and backgrounds, including:

- ○ Gender
- ○ Race
- ○ Age
- ○ Culture
- ○ Experience level

4 Keep Your Employees Engaged

Once you hire talented employees, keep them engaged with processes such as a positive onboarding experience, educational resources, and regular communication. Engage with your international employees so they can help the company grow globally!

RCG

London-based RCG is an integrated market intelligence, management consulting, and technical advisory firm focused solely on the renewable energy sector. RCG's staff of nearly 60 consultants worldwide supports mainstream and emerging technologies, serving the organizations leading the transition to a low-carbon economy.

It serves a diverse clientele with a focus on those where the markets for renewable-energy technologies are strongest: onshore wind, offshore wind, and solar energy. RCG has been transatlantic since the outset, with its first offices in London, Southampton (UK), and in New York, which allowed the firm to hire the best talent in the sector and also be close to its client base. The next step was expanding its service offerings into the Asia-Pacific region with offices in Tokyo and Taiwan.

RCG has offices located all over the globe, from Vancouver to Scotland, Barcelona, and Santiago, in addition to London, New York, Tokyo, and Taipei. However, most offices moved successfully to a remote working arrangement and continue to deliver projects for clients in all regions through its remote-but-connected workforce. Many of these individuals are engaged through Globalization Partners' platform, which enables RCG to minimize the time and cost of supporting its global workforce.

Recognizing that restrictions, lockdowns, and other changes, on top of typical work pressures, were sources of stress and anxiety for its associates, RCG introduced the RCG Bridge program even before the pandemic hit. Senior associates were matched with associates as a way to increase communication and openness internally. It was urged that communications not be about business-related tasks. The program was a success and helped the entire organization through the winter months.

Although the pandemic sparked new programs and ways of working, RCG continued to recruit the best talent. Its expansion plans have not wavered, focusing on those markets where the appetite for renewable energy is the strongest and where it has an opportunity to continue to partner with existing global clients. The business has continued to grow its revenue and remained profitable by adapting quickly to the challenges while delivering ongoing value to clients.

AN OPTIMAL ONBOARDING PROCESS

Although much of the focus when hiring employees is on their interaction with team members and getting them situated with all of the tools and information they need to do their jobs, making sure their payroll and benefits are set up properly is equally crucial—maybe even more so, from the employee's perspective. Because when payroll and benefits go awry and employees, who may be on the other side of the world, have to spend part of their day just getting their insurance set up or fixing the number of deductions they're claiming, they will become disenchanted with your organization very quickly.

Make sure that when new employees begin their jobs, they can focus 100 percent of their attention on doing good work. Don't make them chase down HR reps or have to figure out how to make 401(k) choices on their own. Connect them with everyone on your team who will proactively, quickly resolve all of their benefits questions. Take care of them, especially in their first few weeks.

They'll feel much more a part of the team—an important contributor—if you treat them as if they are a VIP when getting their compensation package worked out. These details should be taken care of with white glove service. This is possible when you work via a competent Employer of Record or hand over the responsibility to your in-country HR and legal team if you're setting up your own branch offices locally.

Of course, most employees also need training regarding how you want them to do their job. They may have the experience and the knowledge to meet or exceed expectations, but your process or expectations may be different than their last employer, so it's important that you invest in everything they need to perform at their best. That means equipment, training, support staff, and budget, if appropriate. Training, at least partly in their time zone, is critical to everyone's success.

There are too many moving parts for a company to be productive when you have a revolving door in your workforce—when an even larger percentage of your costs are attributed to human resources, it's like treading water.

At Globalization Partners, we block off at least the first two weeks of any new employee's schedule and devote it to training. That shouldn't mean that new hires are just sitting at their desk watching training module after training module either. There should be a mix of training content, reading materials, and meetings with fellow employees around the world. In any customer-facing role, a more senior team member should be paired to support the employee with any customer support-related issues for several months while the employee learns the ins-and-outs of the role.

Many departments schedule 15-minute meet-and-greet calls with other department members so that each new employee is exposed to their colleagues and has a chance to get to know them on a personal level. These calls are more about getting to know the individuals and their personalities than talking about work tasks, but having this one-on-one experience can be incredibly helpful when it does come time to reach out and collaborate.

Introducing new employees to other employees is critical. It's a way to connect them to others and to make them feel part of something greater than their individual work. Many of our employees share videos of their home lives, showing their apartments or homes, pets, kids, and their community, to give other employees in other parts of the world a glimpse of what life is like in Belgium, Mexico, or Russia. Giving other employees a snapshot into their lives is humanizing, and seeing a glimpse of another part of the world is one of the best parts of our jobs.

At Globalizations Partners, we've worked to recognize holidays around the world. For example, the whole global team was invited to celebrate Diwali with our office in India. We got to learn about the traditions associated with Diwali and see what it was all about, which was a great way to continue to unify our employees. We also use a platform called 15Five where employees can give a public "high five" to someone to recognize good work that they've done. We use 15Five to encourage every employee in the company to report on what they're doing that week—which is incredibly valuable for a team spanning time zones. My COO spot-checks at least 100 of these each week to understand what's happening across departments. Beyond that, a colleague might type, "Hey, Nadine, great job on that eBook!"

and everyone in the Slack channel can see it. Positive notes inspire other positive notes, and it builds a lot of goodwill and camaraderie.

To keep employees informed and up to date, we share an internal podcast called The Download, which is distributed bimonthly throughout the company. Employees can listen and hear what's going on in the company.

We also hold monthly all-hands meetings in two time zones to bring the entire company together. As we're growing, those meetings are less about me as the CEO talking and more about giving department heads a chance to report on what their teams are working on. We err on the side of sharing more inside information than most companies, but the risk of someone leaving and filling our competitors in on what we're doing is outweighed by the opportunity to involve all of our employees in our strategic goals. I want them to know that they have an important role to play.

Whatever we're doing works—we have a 94 percent internal team engagement score, very low turnover, and exceptionally high Glassdoor reviews. I love my team, and I'm consistently amazed by what we're capable of. Giving our team the love and respect they deserve is returned to the business tenfold. When asked my greatest achievement as an entrepreneur, it's not that we've created a new category; that we built a fully digitized global HR platform that never existed before, or that we've built a multibillion-dollar business that enables any company anywhere to hire employees quickly and easily. My greatest achievement is doing all that while building a business that the customers and employees love. Besides our 94 percent internal employee engagement, our customer service satisfaction is 98 percent.

Beyond the theory, giving new hires what they need to be successful at their jobs also involves discussing in advance what those resources are. Do they need a team? Do they need special software? A large travel budget? What is it that employees believe they require to meet their objectives? It's critical to decide if your business is willing to make that investment on top of the investment of bringing the team member on board.

A number of years ago, I accepted an interim role as the CEO for the North American operations of an Indian company. My job was to bring in new business and capture the North American market, essentially, so we spent a lot of time negotiating exactly what I would need to be successful in this role. After months of careful negotiation, it seemed all parties were in agreement. Yet, when I began to work, I became aware that the promised funds were not available and that the marketing department was severely under-resourced. They didn't want to give me the marketing budget I needed to effectively tackle the market or the support staff to make it possible. These details had been negotiated in advance, of course but simply weren't forthcoming upon actually starting the job.

As you can imagine, hiring a senior executive to grow a business without allocating any resources to support that hire effort is a futile endeavor. I knew I could not be successful given the reality of the situation and didn't want to waste their money (on my salary) or my time. There was no way to be effective with my hands tied, so I had to disengage from the company. Luckily, a gracious ending for all parties was fairly easy to navigate, but I learned a lesson from that.

The point of this story is really to make you aware that you should have these conversations as part of the hiring process, especially when the goal is to tackle a new market, so that everyone is in agreement regarding the total investment being made. Once agreed, delivering on that is critical.

Having had this experience, I knew how important it was to provide team members with sufficient resources, whatever that means for their role. So, when Globalization Partners hired a general manager of Asia, we made sure he had a full marketing team, sales team, and significant marketing budget to achieve his objectives. Obviously, there was no way he could build the business in Asia by himself.

Although we supplied him with the resources he needed, we also relied on him to tell us what would work in the local market. We hired him for his expertise in Asia, so we made sure to listen to what he might need, or how things might be different there. This also is critical. Listening to your local staff is important; they'll understand the local market far better than an executive can from afar.

For example, as the pandemic began to give way in the U.S., thanks to vaccinations, we had conversations with many of our offices, floating the idea that we could all continue to work remotely forever. Many offices liked that plan, but our director in India explained that continued remote work was not an ideal solution there. "We need to get back in the office," he explained. Employees there wanted and expected to be able to leave home and go to an office to work. I suspect that if we had insisted that the global policy was continued remote work, it would have made it difficult to retain and recruit new employees in India. It didn't seem to be the right policy for that area. Ultimately, I trusted him and deferred to his judgment. Moving forward, we will give our team in India flexibility within the local director's guidelines, as well as an office.

Beyond making decisions locally, retaining good employees also requires you to let them know how much you value their contributions and presence. A little gratitude goes a long way, and if someone's dedicating their life to your business, shouldn't they be appreciated?

DIGICERT, INC.

DigiCert, Inc., headquartered in Lehi, Utah, is an American technology company focused on digital security. As a certificate authority (CA) and trusted third party, DigiCert provides the public key infrastructure (PKI) and validation required for issuing digital certificates, or TLS/SSL certificates. These certificates are used to verify and authenticate the identities of organizations and domains and to protect the privacy and data integrity of users' digital interactions with web browsers, email clients, documents, software programs, apps, networks, and connected IoT devices.

With digital security being a global need, DigiCert has expanded its operations to meet demand, resulting in a natural growth of customers and employees across the world. It currently has 1,200 employees worldwide based in more than 15 global locations.

DigiCert's acquisition of Symantec's Website Security and Related PKI Solutions in 2017 marked its entry into the global market. Its 2019 acquisition of the QuoVadis Group, a Qualified Trust Service Provider (TSP) in the European Union and Switzerland, from WISeKey International Holding Ltd., a leading Swiss cybersecurity and IoT company, led to expanded operations in those locations.

Lehi, Utah, and Cape Town, South Africa, are two of DigiCert's largest locations globally. Since the acquisition of Symantec in 2017, the Cape Town team has grown from 168 employees to just over 300 in 2021.

No physical office engagement during the pandemic led to a slightly greater challenge with team and relationship building among the 350+ new employees DigiCert hired in 2020. The effects of remote work haven't been all bad, however. DigiCert employees have had more flexibility and productivity has increased. The team met nearly all its yearly sales and performance targets for 2020 two months early, as a result, and there has been a marked increase in online employee engagement.

Making new employees, wherever they are based, feel welcome has been important. To that end, the TA team partnered with various departments (IT, HR, facilities, and training and development) to ensure that all new employees who are hired (remotely) are given a positive onboarding experience. This is done by ensuring that the team regularly stays in contact with the new hire throughout the onboarding experience. The onboarding plans have also been adjusted to accommodate remote training and onboarding. Although fairly new for many of DigiCert's international locations, to date, the process has proven to be successful.

Express Gratitude

When employees are giving their work their all, it's important to acknowledge them and that level of effort. At Globalization Partners, we recognize that the company has been built by people, and we're grateful for the incredible hard work and talent that they apply every day. We're smarter and more capable than we ever thought possible thanks to the input and ideas that emerge at all levels of the organization. We work hard to encourage that, to let every employee know that their ideas matter, and that we want to hear them.

One way we actively encourage idea sharing throughout the company is through an annual event we call IdeaFest. Anyone in the company can submit an idea for what to do with or for the business. The executive team reviews every idea and then gives out awards. It's similar to another program we have, called the Rockstar Award, which rewards exceptional individual contributors who are nominated by their peers.

Another way that we let strong employees know that they're appreciated and being groomed for future leadership roles is via our Shadow Board program. The executive team picks a handful of people from around the world who have been identified as highly talented future leaders worth investing in. We had our inaugural Shadow Board in 2020.

Those employee shadow board members were invited to a fabulous retreat with the executive team and the board for the kickoff of their project at a once-in-a-lifetime location (imagine a castle in Ireland built in 1,200 AD). The team was given their project and six months later were brought back in to present to the C-suite and board of directors. This gave them exposure to the current company leaders and gave the opportunity to work on important cross-company strategic work.

FEEDBACK IS FUNDAMENTAL

Just as providing professional development opportunities for future leaders is an effective way to begin grooming them for bigger things, it's equally important to recognize when someone isn't working out and to give that feedback as soon as possible, for your benefit and theirs. Employees might have exceptional charisma and a positive presence but simply lack the ability to do their job well. If they are not a good fit for your organization, it's best to let them move on to a role that better suits them, quickly. If you keep them on despite their poor performance, you're potentially communicating to your other employees that doing a bad job is acceptable. It's not.

Successful companies need people who strive for excellence. Because those people then surround themselves with other excellent team members, your whole organization is better for maintaining high standards. Providing regular feedback to every employee is another way to endear them to you and to help them perform at their best every day. At Globalization Partners we do check-in meetings twice a year with the human resource department and one formal performance review a year. But those twice-a-year check-ins are designed to make sure everyone is on the same page and that no one is surprised by what they hear in their official performance review meeting.

When the company was smaller, every employee wrote up a weekly work summary and submitted it via an online software platform. That was probably the best management tool we had because it gave the executive team great visibility into the business. We currently do the same through the software platform, 15Five. Many executives are surprised at the outset that we require every employee to use this software but very quickly appreciate the value of the process because of the visibility they have across the company.

The questions asked within 15Five are: What have you accomplished this week? What are you planning for next week? How is your workload this week? Are there any problems you want to raise to the executive level, or any insights you think would be useful to share? Then employees respond in bullet form for the sake of brevity. Every manager reads their direct reports' submissions, the C-suite reads most of their departments' submissions, and the COO reads at least 100 across the company each week. Getting feedback and regular insight from our employees is critical to our continued success. Of course, we also keep a close eye on our help desk, which gives us critical data to our customer queries and builds their recurring queries into our AI-driven software.

Although you might have heard high-level comments about a particular situation, reading the details from someone who's working hand in hand with customers can be very illuminating. For example, a customer situation that has been reported as a customer service issue could actually be solved via a scalable software solution. The comments are a way to understand the nuances of situations and to recognize when there's an opportunity for positive change. We believe having this type of visibility from our employees (as well as visibility into the questions asked in our AI-based Help Center and customer call listening tools) is critical to constantly improving the company.

Bringing together employees from different parts of the world to work with one another is extraordinary. The diversity of thought and experience can result in brilliant solutions you might never have uncovered on your own. Besides the work product being exceptional, the human experience can be so much richer than working alongside colleagues where everyone has the same cultural background and similar experiences.

Hire the very best, train them well, retain your rock stars, and treat them like gold—and what you'll get back from them will be beyond your wildest dreams. Not only will you retain that top talent, but you'll retain your customers because they will be impressed with the quality of the products and service they receive.

The key to your business success is holding on to that talent, and now, with the ability to hire anyone, anywhere, it's up to you to go find it.

ADDITIONAL RESOURCES

For more information about employee engagement tactics, turn to the following resources: globaltalentunleashed.com/chapter-12

Chapter 13

The World Is Your Oyster

There is nearly unlimited growth potential for companies willing to explore hiring in other countries and expanding into new markets. The truth is, global expansion is possible for companies of any size—there is no minimum revenue level required to qualify to hire a team member outside your own HQ jurisdiction. Companies willing to take that leap often experience revenue growth well above their industry peers, and indeed, often have a lower-cost structure for their talent base to boot.

Global expansion can also be a source of competitive advantage. Being able to hire top talent wherever it is located can provide an unbeatable advantage. In terms of market opportunity, as I've mentioned before, the U.S. market accounts for only 26 percent of the global economy, so even if you move into Europe and Asia, and nowhere else, you've just tripled the size of your potential market. While global expansion is possible for any size business, professionally managed, venture-backed companies committed to maximizing their returns to investors should put international expansion at the top of their priority list. It is an effective strategy for optimizing capacity and resource allocation.

That's not to say that it won't be nerve-wracking, however. Even for major corporations, venturing into a totally new market halfway around the world is anxiety-producing. Hiring employees without having met them in person, thanks to a pandemic, is stressful. But what I can tell you is that hiring local talent in another country when it's appropriate for your business is 1,000 times better than trying to manage customer relationships from afar. It's simply not as effective to be U.S.-based and serving customers a continent or several time zones away. The talent, experience, and ingenuity of everyone has blown me away, time and time again. Hiring the best talent, anywhere you can find it, is the way of the future.

OPEN SOURCE SECURITY

Open Source Security Inc. provides a higher assurance drop-in replacement for Linux, the OS that powers Android and most servers around the world. Its typical customers are in the defense, webhosting, and security industries. Of its six employees, three work remotely from Europe and three work from its headquarters in Lancaster, Pennsylvania.

Going global has enabled the company to hire the best and brightest. The speed at which it can onboard employees makes the whole process seamless, which is especially important for a smaller company like Open Source Security. In the future, the majority of its technical hires are expected to be international.

Although Lancaster is most commonly associated with the Amish and farms, it also has a thriving and expanding tech segment. And if the company were located in a major U.S. city, the founders believe it would still be incredibly difficult to find the caliber of talent the business needs. The technical skills and level of proficiency required for its work are extremely rare: on the order of a few dozen in the entire world.

The company's first international hire was someone who had supported Open Source Security's work unofficially for several years and who happens to be one of the rare few with a strong combination of Linux kernel (OS) engineering and security skills. Being able to hire him and have him continue to work from his home base in Germany was a huge benefit for the company; that employee just completed his first year of employment.

The company has seen most of its hiring success in Europe, where much of its customer base operates, though it suspects location had little to do with it. The company continues to be interested in hiring candidates from virtually anywhere. Great talent exists everywhere, although its leaders have said they wouldn't reasonably be able to access them without a remote hiring capability through Globalization Partners.

Employees in the Lancaster office have worked from home 100 percent since early 2020 following a successful pilot test that ended up becoming pandemic-related when lockdown restrictions were put into place. The local team does miss its dual-monitor setup from the office, the coffee machine, and going out as a group to lunch around town. On the other hand, working from home has had its positives: better availability for family and being able to work in pajamas. Maintaining a good work-life balance has always been an important component of the company, and it's been important to ensure that continues even while working from home. Another advantage of *having international employees is that someone is always available at any time of day or night without having to interrupt a local employee's dinner for a critical issue.*

A disciplined and responsible employee is disciplined and responsible regardless of whether they're working locally or remote.

OPPORTUNITY FOR ALL IS GOOD FOR EVERYONE, EVERYWHERE

Enabling everyone, everywhere, to have access to great jobs via the digital economy is good for everyone. Increasingly, the world is becoming more interconnected. Economies are more closely entwined. Markets are growing more interdependent. That's a good thing.

The democratization of opportunity is the American Dream gone global. The American Dream was always the idea that if you worked hard enough in America, you could make it. Now any talented person, anywhere, can make it. With the advent of global remote work, modern telecommunications infrastructure, and the global Employer of Record industry, the barriers to everyone, everywhere being able to get a good job, have been broken down. This doesn't only affect global talent pools. It's also fantastic for communities in Georgia, Iowa, and Ohio, where our San Francisco- and Boston-headquartered customers are hiring in droves.

Of course, the availability of good jobs doesn't necessarily exist the same way for someone without access to education or clean water, and those situations certainly still exist—and we need to work on that as a society, too. We can no longer have a world where there is such a dichotomy of lifestyles, where some people are wealthy beyond imagination and other people can't find clean water to drink. That said, the best way to address many of the problems of our modern world, whether that's climate change or human migration patterns, is to find ways to provide everyone with access to good jobs in their home communities. Spreading out great job opportunities beyond the 50-mile radius from Boston or the Silicon Valley makes sense for society at large, as well as for employers and individuals. Enabling everyone to have access to opportunity ultimately benefits everyone.

I realize not everyone may see it this way. In the short term, change is scary, especially when we're talking about the availability of jobs when a sizeable percentage of workers in the U.S. are unemployed. Yet it's worth noting that the job market as I write this (in June of 2021) is so hot in the U.S. that salaries are climbing seemingly by the minute—and this is at the new forefront of the era of global remote work. It's also worth noting that international companies are hiring American workers just as much as American companies are hiring international talent—the U.S. is quickly becoming one of our top markets. Nevertheless, the suggestion that American companies should be giving paid work to people in other countries may sound unfair. And yet, providing jobs for people in other parts of the world elevates them to consumer status, making it possible for them to buy products and services they currently cannot, and that they often purchase from the U.S. Those new purchases then create demand, which circles back to those U.S.-headquartered companies, creating new jobs in the U.S. It's a cycle that benefits everyone, everywhere.

Regardless of whether individuals would choose it or not, it's happening—the rise of the rest. Let's embrace the change, and also continue to reinvest in our home communities, and every community we touch, so that we leave a legacy of positivity and opportunity.

> *Global expansion is possible for companies of any size—there is no minimum revenue level required to qualify to hire a team member outside your own HQ jurisdiction. Companies willing to take that leap often experience revenue growth well above their industry peers, and indeed, often have a lower cost structure for their talent base to boot.*

CHANGE IS CONSTANT

The global economy is always in flux. Change is constant. What's true today may not be true tomorrow or next month. It's hard to tell what will change or when. We only know that it will change at some point.

In the 20-plus years that I've been working internationally, the landscape has transformed dramatically. New countries have formed or been renamed, other countries have become popular, and companies now expand globally for different reasons than they did even a few years ago.

However, the opportunities that exist today are far greater than even five years ago, and now companies of all sizes can take advantage of those opportunities. No longer do you need to run a Fortune 500 corporation in order to be able to do business internationally or to hire talent outside the U.S. Any organization of any size can quickly expand its footprint far beyond the U.S., and it's typically easier than executives expect.

The good news is that it is possible for companies to become global players in a matter of months, increasing their customer base, reducing their operating costs, and enhancing the quality of their talent.

All it takes is the confidence and bravery to make that first international hire.

ACKNOWLEDGMENTS

I'd like to thank my husband, Ned T. Sahin, for inspiring me to think big, and for endlessly supporting my endeavor to empower everyone, everywhere. From the hours we spent brainstorming in our think tank in Turkey at the birth of Globalization Partners (GP) and all the years since, you've never failed to encourage me.

I'd like to thank my parents, Rae and Dan, for encouraging me to follow my dreams, even when those dreams led me to adventures that must have been terrifying. From hitchhiking in Brazil to traveling in countries torn by civil war to quitting my job to start a business by myself, you always encouraged me to be who I was. I admire your parenting skills, and I am sure karma is coming for me.

Thank you to every member of my GP Dream Team. Your hard work, ingenuity, creativity, and dedication to breaking down barriers to global business—and for everyone, everywhere—never fails to inspire me.

You proved that we could build a business the way our new generation sees business—not for profit at all costs, but as a way to change the way the world works. We have blown the socks off almost any precedent, from a business metrics perspective, while building a world-class company culture, and a business our customers love. You proved that focusing on a triple bottom line works. We did it, and we are just getting started.

Special thanks to:

- Diane Albano, for creating our revenue dream team, and for inspiring all of us daily.

- Bob Cahill, for breaking the glass ceiling at GP, and for being my long-sought-after strategic CFO who put up with starring at an improv comedy night as part of his interview (and has kept us laughing since).

- Melissa Cooper, for taking a leap when GP was still a dream. Thank you for believing! And also to Steve, who has been an advisory board member from Day 1.

- Jess Dodge, for being a powerhouse CHIEF, team builder, and creator of so many things.

- Michaela Mendes, for your extraordinary magic with words.

- Debbie Millin, for building our business not only with radical competence but also with love. Your legacy echoes through the ages.

- Karen Pantinas, for teaching me how to deliver messages with grace and ease. I could only hope to emulate your effervescent style.

- Francisco Ponce, for capturing the spirit of GP, via your art, music, and style.

- Tracy Schubert, for your friendship and your wisdom.

And to so many more, for your tireless editing, organizing, strategizing, and fact checking:

- Ankit Balani

- Tamrah Buhr

- Jurry De Vries

- Muryel Dias

- Josue Dominguez

- Charlie Ferguson

- Benny Goede

- Nadine Heir

- Kartik Juneja

- Meredith Kelly

- Cynthia Kong

- Claire Lee

- Francisco Mendez

- Thomas Merchant

- Alice Pinero

- Maureen Quinto

- Laura Sullivan

- Noriko Suzuki

- Karen Tan

- Patricia Tan

- Janna Vidal

- Kevin Wang

ENDNOTES

1. https://info.caprelo.com/blog/fortune-500-companies-international-expansion

2. https://chiefexecutive.net/4-real-benefits-from-international-expansion__trashed/

3. https://newsroom.wf.com/English/news-releases/news-release-details/2016/Despite-Weak-Global-Economy-U.S.-Companies-Still-Turning-to-International-Markets-for-Growth/default.aspx

4. https://www.cfo.com/growth-strategies/2020/09/pushing-ahead-with-global-expansions/

5. https://www.bankmycell.com/blog/how-many-phones-are-in-the-world#

6. https://www.linkedin.com/pulse/how-covid-19-has-impacted-different-generations-workers-dan-schawbel/

7. https://www.flexjobs.com/2017-State-of-Telecommuting-US/

8. https://news.gallup.com/poll/321800/covid-remote-work-update.aspx

9. https://lp.buffer.com/state-of-remote-work-2020

10. https://www.owllabs.com/state-of-remote-work/2020

11. https://www.globalization-partners.com/about-us/company-news/majority-of-cfos-indicate-lack-of-global-talent-strategy-will-suffocate-business-growth/

12. https://www.cfo.com/growth-strategies/2020/09/pushing-ahead-with-global-expansions/

13. https://www.oecd-ilibrary.org/sites/e20f2f1a-en/index.html?itemId=/content/component/e20f2f1a-en

14. https://www.bls.gov/opub/mlr/2015/article/stem-crisis-or-stem-surplus-yes-and-yes.htm

15. https://news.gallup.com/poll/321800/covid-remote-work-update.aspx

16. https://www.sfgate.com/local/article/Californians-moving-to-Montana-exodus-tech-16330335.php

17. https://www.worldvision.org/sponsorship-news-stories/global-poverty-facts

18. https://undocs.org/A/RES/70/1

19. https://ubiquity.acm.org/article.cfm?id=2043156

20. https://www.statista.com/statistics/1106711/population-of-europe/

21. https://www.cnbc.com/2020/11/16/rcep-15-asia-pacific-countries-including-china-sign-worlds-largest-trade-deal.html

22. The latest UN estimate as of March 2021

23. https://www.nytimes.com/2013/07/23/world/americas/prices-fuel-outrage-in-brazil-home-of-the-30-cheese-pizza.html

24. https://en.wikipedia.org/wiki/Demographics_of_the_United_Arab_Emirates